Lois Lamplugh

Th[illegible]s

Illus[illegible]
Rich[illegible]

Penguin Books

Penguin Books Ltd, Harmondsworth,
Middlesex, England
Penguin Books Australia Ltd, Ringwood,
Victoria, Australia

First published by André Deutsch 1965
Published in Puffin Books 1972

Made and printed in Great Britain by
Cox & Wyman Ltd, London, Reading and Fakenham
Set in Intertype Times

PUFFIN BOOKS
Editor: Kaye Webb

THE RIFLE HOUSE FRIENDS

What do you do when someone invades your private world? Not many boys would do as Tacker did, but then, as people sometimes noticed, he had an extraordinary imagination.

He had always thought of Miss Lumley's garden as his own special kingdom, so when she had to leave Rifle House, and Sarah and her family moved in, he thought of them as enemies and planned fearful revenges. Certainly the very last thing he wanted to do was become friends, especially when Sarah was given the kind of bicycle *he'd* always longed for. But there were some surprises in store for him, not the least of them the realization that even secret worlds can be shared.

For readers of nine and over.

Cover design by Richard Kennedy

For Susan and Hugh

Contents

One

A Truant in the Stream

Tacker zigzagged slowly upstream. Leggy saplings of ash and alder and hazel topped the hedge on one side of him. The sun shafted through them, throwing tiger-stripes of light and shadow across the water. Now and again, as he moved through a sun-slash, a blood-red flame seemed to spring across his right eye. Interested, he tried to find the exact angle to hold his head so that this would happen repeatedly.

Here on the floor of the narrow valley the still, heavy heat of the summer afternoon settled and brooded. Only the stream was lively and cool, smelled cool, gave off a breath of coolness. Today, just after midsummer, it rippled over its stony bed, so shallow that it scarcely covered a boy's foot; in winter it would rush ankle-deep, even knee-deep in places.

Tacker crouched low and watched the water running over beer-brown pebbles. Infinitely slowly the stream bed was being carried down to the sea; particles of silt and fragments of stone washed along in the current. Here and there among the stones a bit of broken pottery or china jutted out. One china chip, larger than others, caught his eye; he worked it free and found that it was part of a saucer. A few fresh-water shrimps clung to it. He flipped them away and rubbed off a little greenish stain with mud. But this revealed only a few blobby pink and blue flowers; it was a very ordinary cheap saucer. One exactly like it stood on the schoolroom mantelpiece, with a pot plant on it.

At the thought of that drab room where he should now be sitting at a scarred desk, reciting the dates of kings and battles, he sent the bit of saucer skimming upstream over ripple-tips, and curled his toes pleasurably in a pocket of fine silt, so that the stream was discoloured with smoky plumes. It was joyful to be free to breathe the leaf-and-water smell of the meadow, or watch the sky through alder leaves instead of through a window thoughtfully placed high in the wall so that children had no view.

Yet at the back of his mind was the knowledge that he had not truanted this afternoon merely to escape the dread air of the schoolroom. He had done it to spite his mother, because she was in the Rifle House, working for the enemy.

He stepped out on to the bank where, in wet weather, the hooves of cattle cut a trail down to the water. Their slotted, sunken hoof-prints were baked hard in the heavy clay after weeks of sun.

Tacker had been carrying his tattered plimsolls slung over his shoulder by their laces. He unknotted the laces and gave his feet a cursory wipe on a tussock of grass. When he put on the plimsolls he enjoyed the squelch of the canvas against his wet skin.

At the upper end of the meadow a row of tall hedge-top elms threw their shadows across an orchard of little, bent, untended cider-apple trees. Beyond the orchard lay the farm yard, from which came the troubled insistent bleating of sheep. Tacker guessed what troubled them: they were being clipped. He meant to go and watch – from a safe distance, because Mr Veale, the farmer, a sallow, bandy man who had no children of his own, hated boys. To him all boys were marauders, thieves, breakers of hedges and chasers of stock.

And so the village boys roamed his fields and baited him, and tended to leave other less truculent farmers alone. But their forays were mostly over the part of his land that lay nearest to Hamblecombe, the upper of the two valley villages; few except Tacker bothered to come to this distant corner of the farm's western boundary. Tacker found a special spice of gleeful daring in venturing alone on the farm.

Ordinarily he joined in the rowdy, rollicking games of the village children, in the school playground or in the street. No one tried to set on him or set him apart, and although he was small for his age he could stand up for himself. He was not lonely and as a rule he was not solitary. He simply enjoyed going off into the countryside on his own from time to time.

His mother, knowing this, gave him errands to run for her when she could, to distract him.

It was one of these errands that had first taken him to the door of the Rifle House, and a meeting with Miss Lumley.

The Rifle House was a long, one-storey building that had been constructed as an indoor rifle range at the time of the Boer War. In 1914 the range had been useful for the second time as a place where local lads could be trained to shoot. After 1918 most people had become a trifle tired of shooting, for the time being, and the Parish Council, which owned the range, put it up for sale.

It stood empty for a year or so and then Miss Lumley heard it was going cheaply, looked it over, and bought it. She had a ceiling put into the greater part of the building, and rooms partitioned off below – two bedrooms, a bathroom, a kitchen, and a sitting-room with windows looking down the valley. The remainder was left as one enormous room, with no ceiling but a north sky-light, to be used as a studio. Miss Lumley made her living by painting pictures of rocky coasts, thatched cottages, flowers, bowls of fruit, small children, kittens, horses, and cows in sunny meadows. These she sold for reproduction on calendars, birthday cards, and chocolate boxes.

As soon as she had taken possession of the Rifle House, she looked about for a woman to come in on three or four mornings a week to sweep, scrub, dust, and take home her laundry. Mrs Venn, Tacker's mother, presented herself for the job and was engaged.

Mrs Venn gave Tacker the errand of delivering Miss Lumley's clean laundry. He did this for the first time on a windless, yellow-grey November day. When he knocked on the door of the Rifle House nothing happened for a little while; then a window at the far end of the building was pushed open and Miss Lumley's head appeared.

'What is it?' she called.

Wordlessly Tacker held up the bundle of clean washing. He had the advantage of Miss Lumley: he knew her by sight, but she had never noticed him among the racing, darting groups of village children playing in the street as she went by.

'Open the door and bring it along to me,' she directed.

Tacker stepped in warily. He had been inside the building once or twice, through a broken window, when it stood empty, but now that it had become a house, it was strange ground.

He found himself in an entrance hall with a door on his left which, he learned later, led into Miss Lumley's sitting-room. A corridor led down the middle of the bungalow. Doors stood open on either side. From one of them, as he passed, a harsh voice shouted 'Mind your head!'

He glanced into what seemed to be the kitchen and saw a

handsome red and green parrot in a big cage on a stand.

He remembered his mother telling him that Miss Lumley had two parrots. When he came into the studio he saw the second parrot in another cage. This one was grey and scarlet. It regarded him bleakly in silence.

'That's a macaw,' Miss Lumley told him, noticing him looking at it. 'A South American parrot. My father brought it back from Venezuela not long before he died. It's probably older than I am.'

'I saw the other one down the passage,' Tacker remarked.

'They hate the sight of one another. That's why I keep them in different rooms. Otherwise it upsets their livers and raises their blood pressure. If a parrot's blood has pressure. Put the washing on that stool. What is your name?'

'Tacker.' Gaining confidence, he looked directly at her for the first time. She was tall, vigorous, gaunt. Her black hair was greying, even showed touches of white in places. She wore it long, braided and wound into buns, known as earphones, on either side of her head.

She was dressed in a paint-stained brown linen smock over a green woollen skirt, and big, strong, brown leather lace-up shoes. (In summer she wore big, strong, brown leather sandals.)

'Does everyone call you Tacker? What were you christened?'

His proper name was a stranger to him; he hardly ever heard it. He had to think for a few moments to recall it.

'Thomas,' he said finally. 'Victor,' he added, remembering that too.

'Why are you called Tacker?'

He shook his head. He knew the reason. He had crawled at six months and walked at nine. Admiring friends and relations had exclaimed 'Look at the little tacker!' – by which they meant a sturdy toddler. The name had stuck. He had been told this often enough, but would not say it for fear of sounding soft.

'Thomas Victor – Venn?' Miss Lumley asked doubtfully. Mrs Venn had told her that she had two sons and a daughter, but had not referred to any of them by name, or mentioned their ages, and Miss Lumley, absorbed in painting and indifferent to details of family life, had not asked. For all she knew the sons were too young – or too old – to be sent on errands of this sort.

'Yes'm.'

Miss Lumley began to search for something among the books, gramophone records, oddments of crockery, new tubes of oil paint, and pieces of rag that covered a sun-bleached chest of drawers under one of the studio's long windows.

'But you like to be called Tacker, and not Thomas or Tommy or Tom?' she said over her shoulder.

'Yes'm,' he said again. Freed from her attention he gazed about him. An easel commanded the centre of the room, but it had its back to him. A palette and brushes and a scatter of half-squeezed-out tubes of paint lay on a small stained table beside it. On an oak chest near the fireplace stood a gramophone with a big horn that seemed perpetually to listen to all sounds in the room. The only other pieces of furniture were two fireside chairs, a bookcase and a corner cupboard.

The grate blazed red as a night-watchman's brazier with coke, drawing well on a bed of coal, but its heat was swallowed up by the cold air of the studio; it rose into the raftered spaces of the roof peak and was lost.

'Ah, there we are,' Miss Lumley exclaimed, as a small grey suède draw-string purse fell to the floor with a clink of coin. She picked it up and took out a penny, which she presented to Tacker.

'Thank you for bringing me my washing. Did your mother say what I owe her?'

He shook his head.

'Ah, well, I'll ask her when I see her.' Miss Lumley tossed the suède bag back among the muddle and stepped towards the canvas on her easel. She leaned close, scowled, drew back a few paces, and pondered.

Tacker edged round so that he could see it. It showed a scene of cottages under snow, with lamp-light gleaming out and a holly bush in full berry in the foreground.

'For Christmas the year after next,' Miss Lumley explained.

Tacker did not understand what she meant, so he said nothing. This was to happen frequently in his acquaintance with her.

'It's not great art,' she said, as though put on the defensive by his silence. 'In fact it's doubtful whether one may call it art at all. However I enjoy doing it, and people seem to enjoy looking at such things, which is fortunate for me. I'm going to make a cup of cocoa. Perhaps you'd like some?'

She set off down the corridor without waiting for an answer. Tacker followed.

'Mind your head!' the macaw shouted as they came into the kitchen.

'Mind yours,' Miss Lumley retorted. 'And your manners.'

She looked into the sink, where her breakfast dishes, together with tea and supper dishes from the previous day, lay unwashed.

'I suppose I'd better put a kettle on the stove,' she said. 'Then it will be hot by the time I've had my lunch.'

She held the kettle under the tap with one hand and automatically stretched out the other to grasp the short upright handle of a semi-rotary pump fixed at the end of her draining board. Forty feet beneath the Rifle House lay a well that had never in thirty years run dry, even in the long burning summers of 1911 and 1921.

Water splashed into the kettle in jerky gouts. Tacker said, 'I'll do it,' seized the pump handle and worked it energetically to and fro.

'Thank you, Tacker,' Miss Lumley said. She put the filled kettle on a small oil stove and lit the wick.

Tacker went on pumping. Presently a series of heavy, hollow, thudding splashes began to come from overhead. When the pipe leading to the kitchen tap was full, water rose to the tank in the loft.

Miss Lumley glanced towards the ceiling. 'Empty,' she remarked. 'As usual. It takes two hours to fill that tank. I did it once to find out. I was in a mood of unusual doggedness. I doubt very much whether I shall ever do it again. I find it monotonous.'

Interestedly she watched Tacker, who was still ramming the pump handle to and fro. 'Do you like doing that?'

'Don't mind,' said Tacker. 'This un's easy.'

There were advantages and disadvantages in being the only child still living at home, as he was. An advantage was that he now had a bedroom to himself; a disadvantage was that he was expected to help his mother as a water carrier – and as his mother did a lot of washing, she needed a lot of water. In no house or cottage in the parish was water (or, for that matter, gas or electricity) laid on. Washing water, when rainwater butts ran dry, had to be fetched from a dipping place in the stream; drinking water from one of the two village pumps. The long-shafted iron handles of these pumps were a great deal heavier to work than Miss Lumley's newly-installed semi-rotary.

'Is it, though?' Miss Lumley said. 'I suppose you wouldn't care to come down here once or twice a week and pump for an hour? I'd pay you two shillings every Saturday.'

Two shillings! Tacker stopped in mid-stroke and stared giddily at Miss Lumley. He had never possessed more than sixpence at one time, and that seldom. Two shillings a week! He could hide it – save it up – soon he would be able to buy almost anything. A telescope. A camera. A *bicycle.*

'Well, what do you say?' Miss Lumley asked.

He nodded; then managed to find voice to say 'Yes'm,' and went on pumping to show how well he could do it.

'Good,' said Miss Lumley, and set about making cocoa. Having poured it into large pink-tinted mugs which bore the words 'A present from Harrogate', she said 'We'll drink it by the fire. Take this, will you?'

She handed Tacker a tin covered in tartan paper, and herself carried the mugs.

In Tacker's experience cocoa was made with water, like tea, and a small amount of milk added. Miss Lumley's cocoa was in fact drinking chocolate, made with nothing but hot milk, well sweetened. To go with it she offered him a piece of shortbread from the tartan tin. He had never tasted shortbread or drinking chocolate before. For years afterwards he was to remember the surprise of the richness and sweetness of this hot drink and thick crumbly biscuit, as he tasted them for the first time on a stone-grey November morning, sitting close to Miss Lumley's coke-stoked watchman's fire.

Presently, having exchanged sardonic glances with the macaw, Miss Lumley began to talk about her father and his explorations in South America.

'My grandfather had a copy of Raleigh's *Discovery of Guiana* in his Library,' Miss Lumley said. 'My father read it as a boy, and from that time nothing satisfied him until he was able to sail up the River Orinoco, like Raleigh.' Looking directly at Tacker she said, 'You've heard about Raleigh at school, of course?'

Tacker reflected. 'Do you mean that Sir Walter, with the cloak?' he asked.

'That Sir Walter, with the cloak. Precisely. Raleigh was searching for El Dorado – you know, the land of gold. My father was just searching, like most explorers – searching for whatever lay beyond the next mountain. But perhaps everyone who goes on voyages up the Orinoco and the Amazon has a lingering hope of finding El Dorado, even now. Perhaps my father had. I don't know. But South America put its spell on him, that's certain.'

Gazing into the fire she murmured ' "Chimborazo, Coopaxi, took me by the hand." '

Tacker glanced at her, puzzled, and she went on, 'Oh, nothing. A poem that seems to me to express what must have happened to him.'

'Did you ever go there?' Tacker asked.

'To South America? No. All my father's talk of it never fired me to leave this continent. I saw it as a maze of jungle rivers, and I could never remember that those are vast rivers, miles wide for most of their course. My mind's eye saw them – well, sees them still – as deep gorges, full of alligators and anacondas, their banks haunted by head hunters. I haven't the temperament for equatorial adventure.'

She gave the fire a few jabs with the poker and shovelled on more coke.

'My father brought back little enough,' she went on presently. 'Macaws and a tropical disease that killed him long before his time.'

Tacker found this interesting. Everything about the Rifle House interested him. The building itself, the macaws, the paints and brushes, the gramophone, the rich hot chocolate, Miss Lumley and the things she said. He could have sat for hours, half-listening, looking about him, imagining the house was his.

But for the moment Miss Lumley had come to an end. She put down her empty mug and stood up.

Her next remark gave Tacker a jolt.

'I'll speak to your mother about that pumping job. She may not approve.'

'You don't need to tell her,' Tacker said urgently. 'It's all right. She won't mind. I can do it.'

If his mother knew, his two shillings a week, his new fortune, still unearned, would be gone, into a locked money box, saved for him – but not for telescopes and bicycles.

Miss Lumley smiled and suddenly was remote – became an adult speaking to a small boy. 'I'm sure you can, Tacker. But I think I'd better ask your mother first.'

When Tacker, feeling cheated, reached home, he said nothing about the pumping, and still hoped that by some chance Miss Lumley would forget to mention it.

Mrs Venn said 'You've been some time, just taking that old washing down the Rifle House.'

'She gave me some cocoa.'

'She?'

'Miss Lumley.'

'That's better.'

Wonderingly Tacker observed 'She do talk!'

'Ah, her's lonely, poor old duck,' answered his mother, with the comfortable pity of one who isn't.

Two

The Empty House

And now, on this July afternoon, Tacker stood by Mr Veale's orchard hedge, a truant, partly because Miss Lumley had gone. A few yards away a gate led into the long outer yard of the farm, crowded with sheep. Some were pressed against the gate, fleece thrusting through the spaces between the bars. All were agitated; they bleated and panted and covered the trodden, dusty ground with glossy black droppings that quickly became trodden and dusty too. The air smelled of greasy wool.

The flock was too closely huddled to walk through, but even if the yard had been clear, Tacker would not have ventured down it. As scout for a raiding tribe, he could only spy from cover.

He climbed over the high grassy bank into the orchard and ran, crouching, along the hedge to a big rotted-out elm stump, a familiar hiding place. In this cockpit of crumbling wood, spiders and woodlice he ducked down. Here he was between two fires. The back windows of the Rifle House looked out towards the farm; his mother, if she happened to pause in her work and glance out, might see him. And an incautious move on his part might attract the farmer's attention.

He told himself these things, but without much conviction. The thrill of daring that so often came in solitary ventures on the farm was missing today. For one thing, he half wanted his mother to see him, and be vexed because he was not at school. Obscurely he felt that she, who had worked for Miss Lumley, had no business to be meekly working for Miss Lumley's successors, the family who had bought the Rifle House from her: sweeping and scrubbing to make the place ready for their arrival tomorrow. And for another, it was plain that Mr Veale, encumbered with sheep, was in no position to chase a marauder.

Mr Veale sat on a milking-stool in the doorway of a barn, with a sheep between his knees. Its rump was already shorn and the shears were travelling rapidly through the fleece of its shoulders. On another stool sat a second shearer, and between the two men a can of tar bubbled on a small flame, with a branding iron on the ground beside it.

Tacker watched for a while, and gradually tired of it. The late afternoon sun poured down into his hiding-place. Presently sweat began to run down his spine and his skin itched in a dozen places from the bites of what he knew as harvesters: the tiny skin-burrowing mites, harmless but fiercely irritating, that attack anyone working or lazing in summer grass. When they were particularly troublesome, he dealt with them by a method of his own.

The stream's coolness called him back to the meadow by the way he had come. He took off his plimsolls and turned upstream. Soon his way was barred by a tangle of larch poles and wire and blackthorn put across the water where it flowed out, deeper in a narrowed channel, from the corner of the Rifle House garden.

Elder bushes arched from the hedges on either side, heavy with creamy flowers; and a dry stick of elder, stripped of bark and white as a bone, was lodged among some brambles. Tacker pulled it out. It was hollow. Still holding the stick he bent double and edged under the barrier; his chin and the seat of his dingy shorts dipped into the water. Once clear of the dreaded blackthorn barbs that so easily break and fester in the skin, he stood erect. This had been his private domain. Soon it would be enemy territory.

The Rifle House reach of the stream ran in a gulley between a high bank on one side and a high hedge on the other. Where Tacker stood, the bank was at its lowest, only a few inches above the level of his head. Just here grew a big *buddleia variabilis*, now in full flower and haunted by butterflies. Below it Miss Lumley had cut steps in the heavy clay of the bank, and deepened the stream bed so that she could dip out water for her garden: a garden she had laboriously cut from the rough ground that before her coming had surrounded the rifle range. Tacker could see the big orange heads of the oriental poppies she had planted, and the roses on her pergola.

He glanced down. Sunlight flecked the dipping place, and suddenly he saw a sinuous movement, like the apparent rippling of a stick under water. An eel! His hand tightened on the elder stick he held. He was a forest Indian of Venezuela, hunting the river for fish. Poised on his toes, he cast his deadly spear. . . . And the eel flickered and was gone.

His dropped stick began to float downstream. As he grabbed it, water ran out of it as though from a pipe. One end to his eye, the other tilted skyward, he had a keyhole glimpse of mauve buddleia flowers against the soft blue July sky. A blow pipe, better than a spear. Through this he could fire darts tipped with curare. What could he use for darts? Matchsticks? That could wait. For the moment, imaginary ones would do.

He waded forward into the tunnel of green where branches of the elm trees that grew at intervals along the

Rifle House bank reached out towards the hedge-top sallows and hazels and blackthorn opposite. This, in the spring following his first meeting with Miss Lumley, had become the Great Green Gorge of the Orinoco. Here, under water, anacondas lurked. In Tacker's mind anacondas were confused with the conger eels that were caught off the coast and lurked in the huge rock pools on the headland three miles away.

Ferns and ivy, nettles, wild briar and brambles were the undergrowth of his jungle, and around the trunk of the biggest elm a honeysuckle, its bines thick as Tacker's wrist, made a fine tropical liana.

Across the orchard came the constant plaint of sheep. Tacker tried to ignore it. Tame and domestic, it had no place in the jungles of Guiana and Venezuela. He listened to the water voice, which grew louder as he drew near the Great Falls of the Orinoco. On the upper boundary of the Rifle House reach, the stream poured over a lip of rock to fall some five feet, foaming in a deep pool and hollowing out overhangs under either bank.

Tacker stood for a while, holding his hands and arms under the fall. The spray lightly damped his shirt. He splashed water on his face and for a few minutes was free of the burning heat of the afternoon.

Finally he put on his plimsolls once more and climbed swiftly up the bank by familiar footholds. He glanced over his shoulder once, but could not see a face at any window of the Rifle House.

He dropped over a low hedge and was on Mr Veale's property again: in his rick yard, in fact. Old rotted straw was thick underfoot.

Normally Tacker only ventured here in late autumn when the yard was a hamlet of ricks and he could hide in the alleys between them. But today he knew that Mr Veale was too busy with shearing to bother about a raider from the river forests.

The pulpy, yielding, musty-smelling ground was the littered jungle floor. He was coming home to his hut of logs and leaf-thatch – a cart that rested on its shafts inside an open-sided shed – and he was about to climb on to it when he noticed a small, shrivelled turnip lying by one of the wheels.

A shrunken head! He was the witch doctor of the tribe. His hut was set apart from the rest of the village, a dark place of spells.

He sat on the dried mud of the cart floor and took out his knife, an ancient thing given him when his brother acquired a better one. It had half a blade at one end and rather less at the other. He began to carve eyes, nose and mouth on the turnip.

When he was satisfied with it he set up his shrunken head in front of him and stared around. Ahead, half-screened by young elms, was the blank end wall of the Rifle House. The white man's camp! His tribe must be urged on to raid it.

He called them before him and spoke. Stirred by his words, they at once prepared themselves for a ritual dance, and when he held up the shrunken head on his elder stick (now become a wand of power) they began to stamp and shuffle, shuffle and circle, working themselves into a trance of frenzy.

In his mind's eye Tacker had a clear picture of Miss Lumley circling around the easel in her studio as she demonstrated to him the movements of such a dance, movements she herself had never seen and only knew from her father's imitation of them for her amusement as a child.

A sound broke into his Amerindian dream, and the tribal

figures vanished for that day. A grinding rumble was coming steadily nearer. The third and last bus of the day from the market town of Barlingford, eight miles away, was driving up the valley. Tacker watched the hedge gap until the cream and green bus passed. (It still had some novelty; it was only two years since the first bus service to the villages had been started, in 1927.)

He knew that his mother would be relying on the bus to tell her the time, as she had no watch and there was no longer the clock in the Rifle House. For all his defiance, he drew back a little in the shelter of the cart's headboard as he waited.

Five minutes went by, and ten, seeming to him half an hour at least. Then he saw his mother's head and shoulders above the summer grasses of the hedge-top.

He stared at her, and she glanced down at the cart shed and seemed to look directly at him. Her expression did not change and he could not tell whether she had in fact seen him. She went on up the road and the sound of her footsteps died away.

Tacker picked up the shrunken head and his blow pipe. With the latter he shot an imaginary dart at an imaginary jaguar before jumping down from the cart. He looked towards the farm house. Beyond its high slate roof rose fields where white sheep with new black brand marks were beginning to graze. There was no sign of any human being.

Tacker ran across to the hedge dividing the rickyard from the Rifle House garden and climbed through. On this side of the house a door and two small windows led into a cellar cut out of the hillside. He tried the door; it was locked. One window was well secured but the other, he knew, had a faulty latch. He took out his knife, and wished its blades were not broken.

It took him some time to flick up the latch and prise the window open, but he managed it, and climbed through into the cold, clay-smelling, dimly-lit cellar. A few feet away a flight of wooden steps showed faintly.

His heart began to thump. He had been in and out by this way a dozen times, but it was different today, with a deserted house overhead. He scrambled up the steps before his nerve should fail, and thrust at the trap-door above with his shoulders. Was it bolted? Miss Lumley never bolted it. Had his mother, to be on the safe side?

The trap-door gave, and he pushed it back and climbed out into the studio. He took a few steps, then glanced back at the open trap hatch. He realized that he would have to close it if he wanted to stay in the house for more than a minute or two; otherwise bogies would gather in that dark hole, bright summer day though it was. He would be looking over his shoulder again and again, imagining some sound or movement.

He dropped the flap of wood into place by its iron ring, and looked about him. The room, empty, seemed immense. Lozenges of late afternoon sunlight slanted across the floor. No easel, no clutter of paints and brushes and rags, no macaw's cage, no gramophone. Only a faint, lingering oil-paint and turpentine smell. Forcefully it struck home to him that Miss Lumley had indeed gone.

Yet it still surprised him. He had taken it for granted that, having once bought the Rifle House, she would spend the rest of her life in it. But she had a brother in Cornwall who needed her help. His wife had recently died, and he had three daughters to bring up. Although the youngest of these daughters was older than Tacker, Miss Lumley had said, and although they were all useful about the house, she had felt it her duty to pack up and go down to Cornwall to become, as she put it, a domestic aunt as far as she was able.

He stared at the place where the chest bearing the gramophone had stood. That had been the great disappointment: the music. That had been the one thing he could not abide.

On his first visit to the Rifle House he had hopefully eyed the big dark glossy gramophone in the studio, and imagined its horn trumpeting out marches, popular songs, or music hall ditties. These, to him, were music. He was vaguely aware that there were other kinds, but he knew no one who ever listened to them.

For some weeks the gramophone was silent when he was in the house, but one Saturday morning he had a shock. A most tremendous sound was coming from the open windows of the studio as he passed, and indoors it was more staggering still.

Looking along the central corridor he could see Miss Lumley conducting to herself with a paintbrush. He went quickly into the kitchen, shut the door and began pumping with all his might. Soon the satisfactory splosh-splash of water falling into the almost empty tank overhead blotted out whatever it was that the gramophone was doing.

By the time he had finished and Miss Lumley came to make some hot chocolate, there was silence from the studio. He was nervous that when he went along there with her she would start it all over again, but she did not.

He saw, on the label of the record lying on the turntable, the great growling word *Götterdämmerung*, and thought this sounded a very suitable name for what he had heard.

From then on, Miss Lumley played the gramophone fairly often, when Tacker was in earshot, but he went on being baffled by the whole thing. When certain music was played he felt that, if he had been a dog, he would have lifted up his muzzle and howled; other records made him want to go round in circles shaking his ears.

He wondered, now, what the macaws had made of it all; especially the one that habitually lived near the gramophone, at short range, as it were, with no option.

Well, that was over, and no loss – but there were other things he would miss: most of all, Miss Lumley's stories of exploration through danger-haunted equatorial jungles that she herself had never seen.

He remembered the photographs she had shown him of her father. She had a thick album full of pale sepia pictures of an unsmiling man, his face darkened by full moustaches and the shadow of a broad-brimmed hat. Wearing riding breeches and boots he appeared, alone or with Indian companions, against a background of jungle or native huts; sitting in canoes on tropical rivers or, gun in hand, gazing down at some dead animal – puma, jaguar, sad-snouted tapir.

Miss Lumley also had a large map of her father's journeys, on which she liked to point out the places she spoke about. And so, gradually, Columbia, Venezuela and British Guiana became, for Tacker, the only parts of the world, outside the parish of Hamblecombe, that were three-dimensional. At school, geography was lists learned by heart – lists of rivers, mountains, capital cities – as history was lists of dates of battles and kings' reigns.

Miss Lumley did not expect him to listen on an empty stomach. Always, when he had finished pumping, she gave him hot chocolate or lemonade, according to season; and there were biscuits or slices of cake to go with it, and now and then extras from her store cupboard: a handful of seedless raisins, a few glacé cherries and, in the weeks before

Christmas, a piece of candied peel – to Tacker, a delicacy beyond price.

Miss Lumley would go on with her work while Tacker ate and drank, only throwing out occasional remarks. She enjoyed painting as a craft and Tacker, watching, was always fascinated by her skill, and envious of the joyful brilliant squelching mixtures of colour she made on her palette.

When she was elated because a picture had gone well, or depressed because painting suddenly seemed a futile occupation, Miss Lumley would go and work in her garden in great bursts of energy.

Once, splashing upstream after some wide-ranging foray across the enticingly dangerous acres of Mr Veale's farm, Tacker had seen Miss Lumley at work with a hoe, climbed the stream-bank steps, and begun to help. After that he dropped into the habit of doing a bit of weeding in the Rifle House garden when he felt inclined, and Miss Lumley acknowledged this by giving him a penny or two when *she* felt inclined, because this wasn't serious regular work like pumping.

He did not mention these pennies at home – but his early hope that Miss Lumley might forget to tell his mother that she had engaged him as pumping boy had been in vain. Mrs Venn had taken charge of every florin he received (giving him one penny a week for himself, in exchange) and paid it into a Post Office Savings Bank account for him. This remote, unspendable money interested him so little that he had not bothered to ask how much had accumulated.

But in speaking to other village children of his visits to the Rifle House, it was the money he earned that he boasted about. He did not mention Miss Lumley and her talk.

To the village boys she was a figure of fun. They would have considered him daft – and treated him accordingly – if they had thought he found any pleasure in her company. But the knowledge that he earned good money, even if he couldn't spend it, gave him standing.

Tacker had not thought of Miss Lumley when he was not with her, yet his mind had taken on a new colour from the things she talked about. On hot summer days such as this, his equatorial dream had deepened until he walked, half-hallucinated, in a jungle shade, and even in winter his imagination had been livened by ideas of the far half of the world, and his life had been warmer because of her mildly sardonic friendship.

He left the studio. All along the central corridor, blocks of sunlight slanted through doors left open by his mother; he could smell the polish and kitchen soap she had lavished on the house. In the kitchen, the coal-burning range gleamed sooty-bright with blacklead.

Tacker took hold of the pump handle and gave it a few cautious strokes; the sound it made was so loud in the silent house that he moved away hastily. He wondered how many gallons of water he had pumped in the time Miss Lumley had lived in the Rifle House.

He wandered on, and came to Miss Lumley's sitting-room, at the down-valley end of the house. He laid his blow-pipe and shrunken head on the floor in front of the fireplace and sat cross-legged on a window seat. It was the first time he had had a chance to do this, though he had always wanted to.

He rested his arms across his knees, put his head on them, and looked sideways over the garden and the fields beyond. The window faced west. Through the glass, late afternoon sun burned on his arms, legs, and the exposed side of his head. He narrowed his eyes against the flood of light, and at once infinitely small rainbows glinted on his eyelashes. For a while he experimented with this familiar phenomenon, repeatedly squeezing his eyes shut and opening them a fraction to catch the instant at which each separate lash dazzled most brilliantly with spectrum colours.

From this he passed to pressing his thumbs against his closed lids to induce patterns of dots and stars to move against the velvet dark of a feigned blindness.

He forgot everything except the fascination of this game. The crack of a floor-board contracting in the sun startled him back to the present, and all at once he knew how hungry he was. School would have been over for an hour or more, and it was past time he was home for his tea.

Yet he lingered. No one knew where he was, and for this afternoon the Rifle House was his. He revelled in his solitary, secret ownership, and did not want to give it up. Tomorrow the enemy would take possession and this would be forbidden territory; he would not come here again, whatever his mother might do. He would never be a pumping boy for Them – not if they offered him five shillings an hour.

At last hunger began to nag, and he stood up to take one last proud householder's look from the window. Then he picked up blow-pipe and shrunken head and went slowly out of the room.

At the entrance to the long corridor he stopped. Already evening shadows seemed to have filled the studio at the far end – and below lay the dim, earthy cellar. He became aware that, even though he had closed the trap-door, bogies had come, while he sat in the sun here at this safe, light-filled end of the house. They were waiting for him. Against them his blow-pipe was powerless.

He turned back quickly. There was no need to go out through the cellar, after all. What were windows for? He pushed open a sash: then paused as a thought struck him.

He held up the shrunken head and examined it critically. With the better blade of his knife he gave the face a few extra touches of ferocity. This done, he propped it carefully in the centre of the mantelpiece as a sign and warning to the enemy, and climbed out into the sunshine.

Three

A Cure for Harvesters

The Venns rented Bray Cottage, one of the five built on the hillside below the pub and opposite the churchyard. Its windows, three up and two down, stared out at the lych gate; the upper three were on a level with the fuchsia bushes on top of the churchyard wall. The middle one belonged to Tacker's bedroom; in one of its small panes a whorl of green bottle glass appeared perpetually to spin.

Tacker opened the street door carefully. A short dark passage led straight to the back door, the upper panels of which were of thick ridged glass and filtered through a faint green light. He expected his mother to be in the kitchen, a lean-to outside the back door, but the door of the sitting-room opened abruptly beside him and his mother stood there. From her expression, he concluded that she had seen him in the cart shed.

'So you've got down off your chariot,' she remarked. 'And I dare say you're hungry.'

He nodded, eyes downcast.

'Mm,' she said and paused. Tacker recognized that he had succeeded very well in his intention of vexing her, and began to regret it.

'Hungry enough to eat dry bread for your tea?'

This made him glance up swiftly to see if she was in earnest. He could not be sure.

She clicked her tongue irritably. 'Well, it's not ready anyway. I'm late today, after working down the Rifle House.'

He turned to go out again, thinking he had got off lightly, but his mother put out her hand.

'You've been out enough for one day. Wait upstairs.'

And as she followed him along the corridor to the foot of the stairs he heard her murmuring, half to herself, 'Playing truant. I don't know. Playing truant. I've a good mind to tell your father.'

He hoped fervently she would not – but not because he was afraid of his father, whose attempts to lay down the law to him, on the rare occasions when Mrs Venn persuaded him that he must, embarrassed them both.

Tacker thumped his way up the short steep flight of stairs and along to his bedroom. Until this summer he had shared it with his elder brother, Ernie. In April, Ernie had left school and started work as a deck boy aboard one of the holiday-season paddle steamers that sailed around the coasts of South Wales and the south-west of England.

Tacker felt an odd sense of space now that Ernie's clothes, boots, fishing tackle, and treasured bits of machinery no longer took up four-fifths of the room. He had hardly yet made the most of his new freedom to spread out his own few belongings, but the very newest of them hung on the wall where he could see it as he lay in bed.

It was Miss Lumley's farewell present to him: a painting, by herself, of sunset on cliffs at Whittenhoe, the headland three miles away.

He had not seen her at work on it and still found it hard to believe that she had taken the trouble to paint it especially for him; but, looking back, he realized how at odd times she had tactfully drawn from him the sort of painting he would like best to possess.

He went to the window. The sill, deep in the thick cottage wall, was only a foot or so above the level of the floor, a handy place for a boy to crouch and stare out.

A lot went on in this part of the village. At the top of the hill was the high stone-faced hedge opposite the pub where the old men leaned to gossip as they waited for opening time. At the foot of the hill the stream ran out past the end of the churchyard wall and across the road. This was the dipping place, where the women gossiped, while they filled buckets and tall earthenware pitchers, and the younger children dabbled in the water with sticks and rusty cans, and paddled on summer days, and splashed one another.

And all along the other side of the street, but high above street level, ran the churchyard, where villagers processing to weddings and christenings and funerals marked out the progress of life.

Through the churchyard Tacker had come to accept death, since babyhood, as natural and unalarming. He had followed the funerals of his mother's father, and his father's mother, and had been told, often enough, that at three years old, ill with diphtheria, he himself had been close to death.

Looking at the hummocks of eighteenth and nineteenth-century graves, he had a sense that death itself grew old. In old graves like green cots, tucked away in blankets of heavy reddish clay and soft turf, the dead lay dreamless forever.

There were two things in particular that gave him an almost proprietory feeling about the churchyard: one of his grandfathers was buried in it, and the other had the job of sexton.

He rested his chin on his arms and gazed down into the

shady street. Two boys came roaring round the corner by the pub and raced downhill, being motor-cycles. Tacker watched them indifferently. They were cousins of his, but he didn't particularly like them. As the sounds they made died away he heard the leisurely crunch of a labourer's boots on the grit of the road, and his father appeared. His jacket, trousers and cap were as usual grey-white with stone dust. He was a mason; he worked for a builder in a small town not far away.

Tacker looked up at the clock on the church tower. It faced west; its big gilded hands blazed gold in the early evening sun, pointing to a quarter past six. The clock chimed the quarter hour as his father pushed open the street door of the cottage.

Tacker heard his steps pass along the passage below. The back door opened and shut. In his mind's eye he could see his father drop his cap over the hook inside the kitchen door, sit down on a wooden chair, and start to unlace his dusty boots.

Mrs Venn would say 'Hot again then,' and her husband would answer 'Ah, warmish,' and change into an old pair of brown shoes. Then he would take off his jacket and the mud-coloured waistcoat he wore buttoned in winter and unbuttoned in summer, and start to wash his face, hands, and arms at the sink, working up a good lather and blowing as he rinsed it off.

After that – well, after that it was time to eat. Mrs Venn would fill the teapot from the kettle that had been bubbling quietly on a low-turned oil stove for some time, and carry it into the sitting-room where the table was already laid.

Tacker watched the golden clock hand creep down towards half past six. By this time hunger seemed to have taken hold of his stomach and folded it in half. In a few minutes he would know what was to happen. There were several possibilities. His father might come up, looking hang-dog, to deliver a scolding; he might call Tacker down, cuff him unconvincingly about the back of the head, and tell him to go in to tea. Or Mrs Venn might call, give Tacker a couple of slices of dry bread, and tell him to eat them in the kitchen and not let her catch him truanting again.

Tacker opened his bedroom door hopefully. He listened but could only hear a mutter of voices from the kitchen.

His harvester bites began to nag again. He pulled up his shirt and tore at the red pin-points around his waist with blunt finger-nails. After tea – if he had any tea – he would see about them.

Footsteps grated below; the back door opened and his mother's voice, still sharp with annoyance, called up the stairs, 'Tacker!'

'Yes?'

'Come down here.'

He went down, respectfully soft-footed. His parents did not wait for him. They were already in their places at the table when he followed them into the shady, low-ceilinged sitting-room.

Without looking at him his father mumbled, 'You bin missing school again. You do that another time, boy, and I'll belt you.'

'Sit down,' his mother said, and put a cup of tea in front of him.

Still uncertain, Tacker sat down and waited for whatever was to come. On the table was a dish of tinned salmon, cheap pink Canadian fish, but giving off a smell so delicious that he could hardly bear it. It was garnished with rings of hard-boiled egg and radishes from the garden. Alongside was a dish of sliced beetroot. There was also a cottage loaf and a farmhouse fruit cake, both made by Mrs Venn.

She helped all three of them to salmon and began to talk to her husband about a letter she had received that morning from their daughter Molly, who, at sixteen, was in service in Barlingford. She had two days off once a month to spend with her family, and in between times she was apt to write sprawling incoherent letters of home-sickness.

Tacker did not listen. He was absorbed in the act of eating. Gratefully his stomach filled and was appeased. He was hardly able to believe his good luck in being allowed to eat at all – or at least to eat tinned salmon and beetroot with cake to follow. It did not occur to him that his sister's letter had anything to do with his mother's leniency; that, troubled about one absent child, she could feel gentler towards the one still at home.

The threat of a belting was meaningless. There were one or two fathers in the village who occasionally beat their sons with straps; to picture *his* father doing so was unthinkable.

So it was all right. With rising spirits he ate and drank, and when the meal was over helped to carry the dishes to the kitchen.

Then he slipped upstairs to his bedroom again and foraged at the back of a small cupboard built into the wall in one corner. Once this had been Ernie's, but was his private cupboard now, seldom inspected by his mother.

Tacker brought out a little old tin cash box and unlocked it. It contained marbles, a piece of chalk, a foreign coin a summer visitor had given him, some cigarette cards, and two pennies – the last two pennies he had been allowed by his mother for pumping for Miss Lumley.

He put them in his pocket, locked and replaced the box. Noiseless in his plimsolls he crept down the stairs. In the green gloom by the back door he paused to listen. Sounds of washing-up came from the kitchen.

In a minute he was out in the street, the front door closed quietly behind him. Once out of sight of home, he dawdled.

A year or so before, a novelty had appeared outside the village shop: a slot machine. You put in twopence, pulled out the stiff metal drawer and were rewarded with five Woodbines in a green paper packet open at one end. This machine had greatly simplified things for the younger village boys when they set about their first experiment in smoking.

Their only remaining difficulty was where to get twopence, as most of them received a halfpenny or at most a penny a week pocket money. The only solution was to club together. Forsaking sweets for a week, four small boys would contribute a halfpenny each. Their leader would change these for two pennies and wait for a moment when the street was clear. When his followers rejoined him in the chosen smoking place, he gave each a cigarette and kept two for himself, for his trouble. If he was generous he gave the others a few puffs at the fifth cigarette.

Two older boys, putting up a penny each, had an easier answer; they simply halved the odd one.

Tacker had joined Woodbine quartets in his time, but since he had been rich, earning a penny a week for pumping and receiving his usual penny pocket money as well, smoking had somehow lost its attraction. Only once before today had he bought a packet of five to keep and smoke alone, but just now he wanted cigarettes for a special purpose.

Few boys under sixteen ever marched boldly up to the automatic machine. There was always the chance that a busybody would see and tell his mother. Tacker wandered along, watching his moment.

But just because he hoped to see no one, he thought, he had to hang about, pretending to be engrossed in kicking a stone in a circle, while old Tucker went past at one mile an hour on his bicycle, and Mrs Lovering waddled down the road carrying a basket of broad beans, and Gwen Prouse strolled along giggling, with her friend Mary Seldon.

At last the road lay empty in both directions. Tacker ran to the machine, pressed his pennies into the slot and tugged at the metal handle.

Then the green packet was in his pocket and he was strolling homewards, with an overdone casualness that would have made anyone watching him wonder what he had been up to. When he reached Bray Cottage he opened the door softly, crept inside and listened. His mother was upstairs, singing *Under the Deodar* in a fruity contralto. She had sung in the choir until her marriage, and still enjoyed her own voice.

The back door felt warm to the touch from the last of the sun. Tacker rested his shoulders against it. On one side of him was the kitchen, with its lean-to roof of corrugated iron on which, on wet days, the rain drummed loudly. On the other, a tangle of Japanese honeysuckle sprawled over a sagging trellis of old iron-work. Vaguely he remembered lying under the leaves in a green tunnel, when he was about three. That had been his jungle then, in the time when he had known nothing of jungles.

Overhead, through the landing window, Mrs Venn could still be heard singing *Under the Deodar*. In certain moods Tacker listened to her voice with pleasure, and although he could not have put the feeling into words, a song of this kind seemed to express perfectly the gentle melancholy that was part of golden summer evenings such as this.

The singing stopped. Mrs Venn leaned out of the window to call, 'Alec! Just going up to Gran's for a while!'

Tacker heard his father answer from the vegetable plot, and a moment later footsteps came down the stairs and the street door opened and closed. He could imagine his mother walking briskly through the village to the cramped dim cottage where his grandmother lived alone. She would carry an old blue cloth shopping bag, into which, like a middle-aged Red Riding Hood, she always put a few cakes, half a loaf, or some vegetables from the garden, to eke out the food the old woman could buy with her pension.

Bray Cottage garden consisted of a slope of rough grass, with a big stone-built barn at the top, and a large vegetable plot.

Tacker went out to the barn. He paused in the open doorway, then took a few hesitating steps into the dimness. Was it there today? Yes, it was coming. He ducked, arms over his head, and ran out again. White, softly fanning like a great moth, the owl floated out from its daytime perch in the far dark corner, and away over the roof tops. Neither boy nor bird had the nerve to withstand an encounter with the other.

Nothing would have persuaded Tacker to go near the barn after dark, yet he could seldom resist the thrill of venturing into the place by day. Often the owl's perch was empty, and he would cross the floor and stare up at it – a dusty rafter, spotted with droppings – and imagine the bird was there, tame; his bird to call to his finger or carry on his shoulder.

Tacker went along the side of the barn. Built on to the back of it was some kind of small outhouse, also of stone, disused and grown about with nettles. Its roof had long since fallen in, and in places the mortar between the stones was crumbling.

In the summer after he had learned to walk, Tacker had

discovered and explored this place. In spite of stings from its guardian nettles, he had kept on until he somehow pushed and stamped a way into the little ruin, and sat on its slate-cluttered floor. It was one of his first clear memories: sitting in the weed-grown space and staring up at the rectangle of hot blue sky enclosed by the roofless walls, with swallows wheeling across it.

After that he had gone often to this secret house that no adult bothered with. As he grew older he gradually cleared away the fallen slates and weeded and smoothed the earth floor beneath. In one corner he built a hearth of stones, and brought out an old wooden box for a seat.

Nowadays he felt he had rather outgrown the ruin, and did not often visit it. But it had one special use. He had long ago discovered a loose stone at the foot of the wall on one side, where it joined the barn. One day, having something he wanted to hide, he removed the stone and dug a hole beneath the place it occupied, large enough to take a tobacco tin. This tin had acted as a private safe ever since. The cupboard in his room was all very well, but could not be reckoned wholly secure and secret.

The doorless opening of the ruin was screened from the vegetable plot by a cluster of elder bushes. Having made sure that his father was still at work on the plot, Tacker went quickly to his safe, put the packet of Woodbines into it and replaced the concealing stone.

Then he wandered along the cinder path to the potato rows that his father was 'heeling up'.

'Shall I help you then?' he offered. Only like any boy of that region, the way he said it sounded like 'Wull I 'elp ee then?'

'If you'm mind to,' his father assented. 'Hoe they cabbages, will you?'

Tacker fetched a hoe from the tool stack just inside the barn and set to work.

The only sign his father gave of his pleasure in his son's company was that he began to whistle, tunefully and with great sweetness, *The Farmer's Boy*, which was the song he always sang in the village pub on special occasions.

Father and son worked together in amicable silence until the potato heeling was done. Then the man straightened and stretched, and stared up for a few moments at the swifts that had flashed and dipped and swerved over the village all the evening. They were flying high because the midges they fed on were flying high: it would be another fine, warm day tomorrow.

The church clock chimed the half-hour: half past eight.

'I'm going up the road,' Alec Venn said. 'You'll be all right? Your Mam'll be back soon.'

Tacker muttered that he would be all right. The question was only a formality; it was no new thing for him to spend an hour or two in the house or garden alone, especially in summer.

His father tramped away towards the cottage. Tacker finished the row he was on and went to put the hoe away, trying to copy his father's leisurely, measured tread and crunch the cinder path as he did. But in plimsolls it was impossible to get the right, satisfying sound.

He searched around the garden, under bushes and the crooked old apple trees that edged the vegetable plot, for dry twigs and bits of stick. With a handful of sun-burned grass as kindling he built a small fire on his stone hearth in the ruin. In the tobacco-tin safe he always kept a box of matches. He took this out and lighted the grass. A little flame ran quickly along the hay-dry stems and the smallest twigs began to catch.

Tacker crouched and watched the fire; he dropped on more sticks until he was sure it was well alight. Then he sat back, took a cigarette from the tin and lit it with lingering care.

He leaned against the barn wall and tilted his head back, watching the swifts as his father had done. He drew smoke into the back of his mouth, held it, and breathed it out again.

The fire was camouflage. If his mother should happen to return earlier than expected and come to look for him, the cigarette could be dropped into the flames and its smell would be lost in the woodsmoke smell.

Now it was time to treat his harvester bites. He pulled up his shirt, drew on the cigarette and for an instant held the glowing end as near one of the pin-point marks around his waist as he could bear. The faint burn extinguished the irritation, and he passed on to the next and the next, only pausing to draw on the cigarette. He knew from experience that the heat of the tobacco ash acted as a counter-irritant to the itching of the bites and actually seemed to cure it completely.

Soon he had treated every mark on his body; the cigarette was down to an inch-long stub, and blissfully there was no more itching. Satisfied, he smoked the stub until he could no longer hold it, and dropped it into the fire.

He opened his tobacco tin again. Should he have a second cigarette? Perhaps not. He laid the paper packet and box of matches back in the box and looked at the only treasures hidden there at the moment: three tubes of oil paint. One small and unused; the others, the crumpled and three-quarters empty remnants of larger tubes.

The new one was Alizarin Crimson; the others, Mid-Cadmium and Cobalt. He had stolen the Cobalt on one of his

early visits to Miss Lumley. He watched her squeeze out the rich blue on to her palette and quite simply coveted it. She often had one or two tubes of the principal colours she happened to be painting with in use at once; he was fairly sure that the old tube would not be missed, and he was right.

Because she let him try his hand with her paints and brushes, he forebore to steal any more from her until he learned that she was leaving. He took the Cadmium on the day she told him the news, and defiantly, slid the Alizarin Crimson into his pocket while she was in the room, not long before she said good-bye. He had often wondered since whether she knew, and suspected that she did. Because she had not said or done anything about it he felt sorry for this theft.

The fire was dying and it was growing dusk. A dark shape

flickered overhead; no swift this time but a bat. A flittermouse, Tacker called it. Soon he saw another, and another. He heard their first midget slate-pencil squeaks as the screams of the swifts grew fainter.

Soon his mother would be home, telling him it was time for bed.

He took off the cap of the tube of Alizarin Crimson and looked at it in the ebbing light. The lovely brilliant colour was useless to him, since he dared not even daub it about on the stones of the ruin, as he was tempted to do, lest his mother see it and question him.

The smell of oil paint brought vividly back to him the studio on warm days like this, with Miss Lumley working and talking. And then he remembered the big empty room as he had seen it a few hours earlier, and a summer evening melancholy more intense than he had ever known swept over him. For the first time in his life he had a desolating sense of the ending of things.

Four

The Rickyard Spell

For two weeks Tacker spent his spare time in the street with the boys of his own age. The village school closed for the summer holidays and the children roistered in the warm free days. They brought out wooden boxes on wheels, pushed them up the hill by the Queen's Head, and trundled triumphantly down; they bowled iron hoops; they ran around with tin cans on strings trailing at heel. They shouted and fought and splashed in the stream where it ran along the churchyard wall. They went roving over the fields to a little neglected orchard of cider apples, and ate the sour fruit. They hunted along the hedges for the first ripe blackberries. They ran errands to the shop for their mothers, when they had to, and bought great gob-stoppers, four a penny, which changed colour as you sucked them, layer after layer, shade after shade, to be examined every few minutes, a pleasure both to the taste and to the eye.

Tacker ran wild, with the wildness of the pack. He had several fights, gave black eyes and gained one, tore his clothes, cut his knees in falls, and lived through the boisterous hours in a haze of restless, mindless energy.

And then, suddenly one Sunday evening, he tired of it, and went off alone after tea along the shore road, once a lime-burner's track, that led down to a disused kiln on the edge of a wide sweep of sand.

This road had never known a macadam surface. It was made of red, iron-rich stone, like many of the minor roads in the district.

From either hedge the grasses grew long and heavy with seed. The rare passing car would brush them, clipping off bents to drop into the laps of its occupants. Field scabious, poppies and the tiny yellow-snapdragon heads of toadflax swayed among the grasses.

The road curved, rose a little, levelled and began to run downhill, and far ahead beyond the fields lay the sea, glittering in the late sun. The high dark cliffs of Whittenhoe ran out due west for more than a mile.

Tacker could not swim, and had never been down to the beach simply to picnic and spend a summer's day. Village children didn't. Bathing and lazing on the sands were things holiday visitors did, or a few local residents who had private incomes. Villagers were too busy. If they went to the shore it was for a purpose: to set lobster pots, to fish, to collect laver, the edible seaweed, or driftwood for firing, or a load of seaweed to manure the garden. Tacker had come down with his father, pushing a home-made hand cart, after some of the great gales of the autumn equinox, to haul home a few hundredweight of bladder-wrack and oarweed for the vegetable plot.

Suddenly, as he meandered along, he heard the soft putt-putt-putt of a Trojan car engine. It was coming up from the direction of the beach. He saw a gateway some yards ahead and ran to it: there was no room for pedestrians and cars in this lane.

From the safety of the gateway he waited to watch the car pass. Its waterproof hood was folded back and he could have put out a hand and touched its occupants as it went by – a man, a woman, and a girl about Tacker's age. To them, he was just a nameless village boy, as far as they noticed him at all; to him they were the enemy. They were the Wickhams, the new owners of the Rifle House.

They had the sun-flushed look of people who had been on the sands all day. In the back of the car with the child were two dogs. Tacker had heard about these from his mother, who was now working for the Wickhams on three mornings a week, and so knew that they were Corgis, a breed he had not seen before.

He watched the Trojan until it putt-putted out of sight on its solid tyres, scattering grass seeds. Then he climbed over the gate and walked away from the road.

Ahead of him rabbits bounced towards their burrows; farther away they stopped feeding and froze, waiting to see what he did. Farther away still, where the pasture ended in steep furzy slopes, they went on browsing over patches of grass. Twice he noticed the ferocious iron fangs of a trapper's gin, half-buried in loose soil in the hedge bottom.

He came over the brow of a hill and there far below was the other shore road, the one that ran down, following the windings of the stream, to the bay that lay south of Whittenhoe.

The steep shoulder of hill on which he stood was covered with a patch of bracken and gorse. Among the bushes were little islands of rabbit-bitten turf dotted with droppings.

This was a place in which to lie, watching kestrels hover and drop like stones on their prey, or buzzards swing over the valley (one year they had nested in one of the oaks on the slope below but he had been too small then to dare to climb to the nest), or gulls drift down the sky at evening, gliding on warm air currents, their wings dazzlingly white against the clear blue.

It was a piece of waste, neglected ground; a corner of the farm that Tacker regarded as his own. He had never come across anyone here.

He climbed over the hedge-mound in front of him and went down through the oak copse.

Presently there appeared, through the trees, the mellow russet roof of the Rifle House, and he knew why he had left the shore road and come this way: to spy out the land. He had not been near the Rifle House since his truanting day, but through his mother he had learned a good deal about its occupants and their dogs and their plans for the future. She had told him nothing directly; she knew his partisan feelings about Miss Lumley too well. But on the days she worked for the Wickhams she chatted to her husband, over the tea table, about the newcomers. On the strip of level ground behind the house, that had been Miss Lumley's potato patch, they were having kennels built and runs of chain-link fencing put up. The two Corgis Tacker had seen in the car were to be followed by others. The Wickhams intended to breed and board dogs.

'Do you reckon it'll pay?' Mrs Venn asked.

Her husband shrugged and said that it sounded to him a diddly old business.

Tacker decided to put up a witch doctor's spell on the undertaking; on the Wickhams' side of it, at least. He didn't want to ill-wish the dogs.

Below the copse lay a strip of pasture, the westernmost corner of Mr Veale's property. Tacker ran across this to the shelter of a line of big elms. From here he could see part of the Rifle House garden. Had the Wickhams reached home yet? There was no sign of them, but they must be there unless they had stopped somewhere along the road.

A few moments later he was ducking carefully under the

wire and blackthorn barrier that divided the little meadow from the Great Green Gorge of the Orinoco. He stood on tiptoe and looked again at the slope of Miss Lumley's garden, a bright confusion of the flowers she had planted. Still no sight of the Wickhams.

To see the new kennel buildings he would need to go upstream and climb the bank where it rose higher.

Deep in dangerous territory near the white man's settlement, he waded slowly, barefoot, a wary Indian ready to run for the shelter of the jungle.

At the first bend of the stream a young elm grew out from the bank; he pulled himself up by this until he could stand in the curve of the thin trunk. Now he could see the ground at the back of the Rifle House, cleared and levelled, and on it, concrete foundations, stacks of timber, and rolls of chain-link wire-netting.

The windows all along this side of the house stood open. He heard a room door slam; a man's voice called something. He ducked – and heard another sound from somewhere near the Great Falls of the Orinoco.

He slithered back into the stream, nearly dropping his plimsolls, and rounded the second bend even more cautiously. Suddenly he stopped and stared.

The bank ahead, just below the waterfall, had always been a shady place of fern and ivy, with brambles higher up. Now light shafted down on the pool below the falls; the brambles had been overlaid by a tip of earth and stones. And part of the bank itself had been sliced away to make way for a strip of path a few inches above the water. On this strip stood the girl he had seen in the Trojan. She was raking stones from the bed of the stream, evidently to use as foundations for the next stretch of the path. It was the raking sound Tacker had heard.

He watched her, astonished and outraged. She was *changing* the stream – *his* stream. This piece of it had been his for years, even before the coming of Miss Lumley, and he had left it alone. And Miss Lumley, although she had carved a garden from the rough ground around the old rifle range, had done no more to the stream than cut steps in its bank to enable her to dip out water.

The girl became aware of his gaze and looked up. He stared at her with the malevolence of a cat sighting a rival. He forgot caution and moved nearer. Sheer indignation overwhelmed him.

'Gar, you think you *own* the place,' he said, and he knew what he meant, although he realized that he wasn't putting it very well.

At first the girl said nothing. Startled by the suddenness of his appearance and the ferocity of his expression, she could only gaze at him in bewilderment. Who was this rough-haired invader? What was he doing here and why was he so angry? She had not noticed him on the shore road, and although she saw Mrs Venn two or three times a week, she had no idea what her son looked like.

She resisted an immediate frightened impulse to run to the house and tell her parents that a weird village boy was trespassing in the garden, and told herself that it would be silly to be afraid of someone no larger and probably no older than she was.

'What do you want?' she managed to say. 'What are you doing here?'

'I *belong* here,' Tacker told her forcefully. 'I bin here for years.'

'Here? How could you have been? And what did you mean, I think I own the place? Of course I don't. My father does, though.'

'What are you doing to the stream, then? That!' He pointed to the stretch of path.

'I'm going to make a path all along the part of the stream in our garden.'

'You *can't*!' he protested, envy now mixed with outrage. If only he had built himself a private track along the Great Green Gorge!

'Yes, I can. It's hard work, but I'm going to do it.'

'I'm going to do it,' Tacker mimicked her, in a fury. At that moment, from one of the windows above, a woman's voice called 'Sarah! Sarah, where are you? Supper!'

The girl called back 'Yes. Coming.'

Tacker said sharply, 'Don't tell 'em about me.'

'Don't be silly,' she answered, turning away and beginning to climb the bank, and he could not be sure whether she meant he was silly to think she would tell, or silly to think she wouldn't.

And now for the first time it occurred to him that the Wickhams must on no account see him and associate him with his mother. If she heard about this trespassing escapade, there would be no end to it. There was even the terrible thought that the Wickhams might blame her, or hold her responsible for his behaviour.

Keeping his head down, as though if he didn't, Mr or Mrs Wickham might by some X-ray process see through the back of it, he scrambled up familiar footholds at the side of the waterfall, jumped into a rickyard and ran, stooping, to the cart shed, without so much as a glance towards the farmhouse. Mr Veale was the lesser of his enemies at the moment – and in any case, at this time on a Sunday evening, would probably be in Hamblecombe, visiting his mother.

Could he find another turnip to make a shrunken head? He poked about in the mushy straw floor of the yard.

No turnips, but he saw a twisted thatching peg dropped from a dismantled rick; then a length of twine, flossy with age. He took these and a handful of straw, and went back and sat on the cart and twisted and tied straw around the peg to make a malign, spell-binder's doll.

When it was finished he sat with his legs crossed, swaying from side to side in a witch doctor's trance, putting a curse upon the straw doll. And as he did so, somewhere at the back of his mind was the voice of Miss Lumley, talking about Amerindian jungle spells, as she had heard of them from her father.

Then he took the doll to the stream bank and dropped it in. It slid over the glassy curve of the waterfall and vanished. He could picture it bobbing in the miniature whirlpool at the foot of the fall, and eddying gradually outward until the current took it and carried it down. Somewhere along the Rifle House reach of the stream a claw of briar or bramble, swaying at water level, might clutch and hold it until Sarah Wickham came that way and saw it, and picked it up.

Five

The Trap

The day after Tacker's encounter with Sarah Wickham, something unusual happened. He received a letter.

Mrs Venn picked it up eagerly from the mat, hoping it might be from Molly or Ernie. She was always hoping for a letter from Ernie, who in fact never sent more than a few scrawled words on a picture postcard of Cardiff or Swansea. Disappointedly she stared at the large, squareish, well-spaced handwriting on the envelope, addressed, so improbably, to Master Thomas Venn. Certainly not Ernie's, yet somehow familiar; she had received messages in this writing half a dozen times. It was Miss Lumley's.

In silence, but with a vague feeling of indignation, she handed the letter to Tacker, who was finishing his breakfast.

He stared at the envelope and then at her, half suspecting some kind of joke – for who would write to him? But his mother sat down at her place and ignored his questioning glance.

'What's that, then?' his father asked.

'Letter,' said Tacker helpfully, looking at the Cornish postmark and beginning to guess.

'Miss Lumley,' Mrs Venn put in.

'She can't be all that busy down there, looks like,' Alec Venn said. 'If she's got time for letters.'

He gulped his tea. 'I'll be off up the road then.' He picked up his cap, flopped it on the back of his head, gave it a twist to settle it, and clumped out.

Tacker opened his letter. A square of cartridge paper fell out. He picked it up and saw that it was a pencil drawing of a harbour wall and fishing-boats, with the initials D.L. in one corner. He pored over it for a while, admiring each delicate detail; then propped the drawing in front of him and turned to the letter itself.

A halting reader of print, he ordinarily regarded handwriting as a language beyond him. But Miss Lumley had guessed this and, to avoid the insult of capital letters, had tactfully used a large clear italic script; he found he could read this at least as easily as the books at school.

Dear Tacker,

You are in the midst of your school holidays, enjoying the weather and the freedom. I am pretending to be a housekeeper, but I find that my nieces are better at all of it than I am, especially cooking. At school they do Domestic Science, which is apparently school language for housekeeping, a subject I was never favoured with in my youth. In consequence I feel a bit of a fraud. As my nieces have kindly given me the afternoon off, I am sitting in the sun writing letters. I was going to send you a picture postcard of the village, but I started to scribble a few views of the harbour, so perhaps one of them will do instead.

There are painters here of all kinds – mostly my kind, I fancy.

(But what other kind was there, Tacker wondered.)

I have set up my easel once or twice on my afternoons off.

I miss Hamblecome and all my friends there. But no doubt I shall be able to come back for a visit one day.

She signed herself Dorothea Lumley. The first name surprised him. He had never thought of her as possessing one.

With some impatience Mrs Venn watched him absorbing his letter, word by word.

'Well, how's Miss Lumley?' she asked, when he looked at last to be near the end of it.

'She says she's not doing much cooking. And she wants to be – ' he hesitated over the word ' – remembered to you. Remembered? What does she say that for? You wouldn't have forgotten her so quick.'

'It doesn't mean that.' Mrs Venn began to clear the table. 'She won't be sorry about the cooking, I know. My dear soul, she didn't care for any sort of work around the house. Who's doing the cooking then?'

'Her nieces.'

'Oh, yes, well, so they should. One of 'em's as old as our Molly, nearly, and the other's not far off old enough to leave school. Though of course that sort stays on till they'm grown up, just about.'

She scrutinized the pencil drawing. 'That's pretty. You could frame that.'

She began to stack up dirty dishes.

Tacker went up to his room. He pinned the drawing to the wall near 'Sunset on Whittenhoe', and put the letter away in his cash box. For a moment he stared from his window. Out in the street his cousin Archie Snell raced downhill, towing a string of tins, followed by three slightly younger boys.

Tacker rushed down the stairs to begin the outdoor day.

It was a warm, still morning, but in the afternoon a chill air drifted across the hillsides. Sea mist was moving in with the tide, creeping along the coast and up the valleys. The fog-horn on the headland to the north of Whittenhoe began to bellow mournfully.

Gradually the village was submerged, as though it had entered cloud.

Tacker and half a dozen other boys were kicking about a flabby grey tennis ball, left behind by some summer visitor, on the wide, level stretch of road below the dipping place.

When they heard a car coming they scattered. Its engine purred gently, putt-put-putt, as it rolled cautiously along the curving, misty street. Was it the Trojan, Tacker wondered, as he stared towards the sound. Yes – there was Mr Wickham, alone this time, but again with the hood down. Instead of driving past, as the boys expected, he stopped in the midst of them.

'Any of you seen a dog straying about?' he asked. 'One of my Corgis? You know what they look like, don't you?'

He gazed from face to face. In silence the boys stared back – all except Tacker, who edged round to the rear of the car and looked at no one. His first, jubilant thought was that the spell had worked; his second, remembering his resolve not to ill-wish the dogs, that it had worked the wrong way.

Mr Wickham tapped his driving wheel.

'Well, hasn't anyone got a tongue? Haven't any of you seen the dog?' His voice hardened. There was a rumour that until recently he had been an Army officer; that he had received a legacy and bought himself out.

He fixed Archie with a compelling eye. 'What about you? Anything you can tell me?'

Archie managed to say, 'I aren't seen no dog,' and at this the others chorussed that they hadn't either.

'All right. But if anyone does, let me know as soon as possible, won't you? His name's Budge. I'll make it worth your while.'

He drove off and the boys strung out across the road again, and capered and shouted mocking remarks, and mimicked Mr Wickham's voice and manner.

Only Tacker stood where he was and said nothing. All day he had been plunged in the wild, mindless world of street play. The mood in which he had made the straw doll and dropped it into the stream was unreal to him now; the boy who had done that was someone else. The spell had been nonsense – it couldn't have worked. And yet he felt twinges of guilt and fright.

He drifted away from his companions. Archie called after him, 'Where you going?'

'Up home a minute,' Tacker muttered.

'You got that little old dog hidden away in a cupboard?' another boy shouted, and they all laughed.

Tacker did not answer. Indoors there was a warm sweet smell. His mother had been making jelly from crab apples given her by a neighbour.

A row of jam pots filled with clear reddish-amber jelly stood on the kichen table. Mrs Venn was tying covers on them. Supposing that Tacker had come in because he was hungry, she buttered a crust and spread it with the sticky testing jelly from a saucer.

Tacker accepted this unexpected titbit gratefully, and sat in the doorway to eat it. He wondered whether his mother had heard yet about the Wickham's lost dog. It was not one of her days for working at the Rifle House, but the village bush telegraph might somehow have brought her the news by this time. He wanted to ask her, but guilt gripped him.

Presently she sensed that he had not come in simply for something to eat; that he was in fact hanging about.

'Anything wrong, Tacker?' she asked.

'No,' he said anxiously.

'Feel all right, do you?'

'Yes.'

'Nothing wrong with your appetite, anyway.'

'Mr Wickham stopped down the road just now,' he blurted out, losing his nerve.

'What for?'

He told her, and she looked at him consideringly, trying to make out why he had been bothered by this happening.

'One of they little dogs lost? Which one?'

'He said it's called Budge.'

'Oh, yes. Pity. In this mist, too. People leave the gate open, that's the trouble. Mrs Wickham told me it's always a worry – especially here, where the dogs are strange. Worth a fair bit of money, they are. Well, you'd better go out and see if you can find this one, hadn't you?'

For the first time since he had come in, he met her eyes. Was it as simple as that?

He scrambled to his feet. 'All right,' he said, and ran out.

The others were still kicking the ball about at the foot of the hill.

'Ay, Tacker!' one of them shouted, but he called back, 'Can't stop,' and went up the street and out of their sight.

He felt released. There were no spells, only people leaving gates open.

In the forge, a dark, fire-lit cavern dug out of the side of a hill, the blacksmith's hammer rang like a bell. At the forge the village ended – and today it ended in nothingness. The valley had vanished. The countryside in the mist was an under-water world; trees loomed up like kelps and dulses and brown sea-wracks in the Atlantic tides. All sound was muffled, except the bellowing fog-horn.

Tacker climbed a field gate. To keep to the road would be useless; Mr Wickham had been that way in his car. He tried to imagine where the dog might go.

He went steadily from field to field, sometimes called 'Budge! Budge!', sometimes stopping to listen. He knew every acre of these hillsides and could hardly have got lost on the darkest night. From each mid-field he saw the blurred shapes of hedges, softly cocooned in fog. On an ordinary bright summer afternoon he would have been able to look far away across the farm lands; any small reddish-brown dog, foxily running over the grass, would have been easy to see.

Today nothing but chance would help him. Or one sound – the sound he listened for.

He was on a hillside above Combascott before he heard anything, and then it was a shrill thin screaming, not a dog's cry. The high terrible screams pierced the mist like silver needles. Tacker followed them until he came to the trapped rabbit.

Like any country boy, Tacker thought nothing of killing a rabbit. Ordinarily he would have knocked this one on the head and hidden it somewhere near the village until he could return with a bag or basket in which to carry it home for the pot, and no questions asked – not even by his mother, who would accept this sort of poaching once in a way without scruple. But this evening he was conscious of being on an errand of mercy. He bent to gauge how badly the rabbit was injured, and decided that its lacerated leg stood a chance of healing, though the creature, frantic with fear of him, looked likely to sever it by its desperate tugging to break free.

Tacker had been taught long since how to release the jaws of a gin. He trod on the spring and the rabbit bounded away, fell, rolled and lolloped one-sidedly towards a burrow.

No one Tacker knew would have approved of what he had done. They would have said 'Knock it on the head and have done.' Rabbits were vermin to be rid of – and in any case, if released with an injury, would die a slow, miserable death or be set upon by its fellows.

But Tacker had more than once seen a rabbit, alive and hearty, lacking a paw; he knew they *could* survive after a trapping.

He went down into Combascott, and thought of asking at the shop if anyone had seen the Corgi, but reckoned that Mr Wickham would have done that already. He wandered through the village looking into people's gardens, and then took a lane that led to the old lime burner's track.

Heading back towards Hamblecombe, he quartered field after field, peering into the mist and listening again.

'Budge!' he called. 'Budge!' But the name seemed sillier every time he said it. He tried whistling, and the thin sound was swallowed up by the soft, bemusing mist. He was hungry by this time.

Faintly he heard the chime of the church clock and counted the strokes. Seven o'clock. He trotted across the field he was in. The bars of its remembered gate appeared in the dimness. He climbed over and was in the road. In ten minutes he was home, and his mother saw from his face that he had had no luck.

'Never mind, perhaps they'll find him when the mist takes up,' she said. 'Come and have your tea now. I've kept it for you.'

When he woke soon after six the next morning, the light at his window showed winter-pale. He peered out and could not see even the top of the church tower. The regular roar and pause of the fog horn still came inland from its cliff-top like the cry of a great stranded animal.

After breakfast Tacker went out. He did not mean to search any more. It was his mother's day for going to the Rifle House. At midday she might bring back news; perhaps the dog had been found.

He wandered eastwards out of the village, uphill towards the source of the stream, away from the Rifle House.

The spring bubbled out of the ground, spilled down a bank into a ditch and ran beside the narrow road until it disappeared into the Rectory grounds. Early in their acquaintance, Miss Lumley had asked Tacker where the stream rose. When he said he didn't know, she was quite sharp with him. 'Of course you know. You must know. You live here, in this valley,' she told him.

At their next meeting she perplexed him momentarily by saying 'Well, I have been to the headwaters. I have traced the source of our Orinoco.'

As she went on to describe where she had been, he realized what she was talking about; he realized also that she had been right in saying he had known all the time where the stream rose. He simply had not connected the roadside water-splash with the later course of the stream.

Past the water-splash, past the high banks grown with gorse, past cows to be heard breathing and chewing but invisible in the mist in fields seven or eight feet above the roadway, he climbed until he came to a point from which, on clear days a great view of bays and headlands, distant estuary, villages and hillsides opened out. Here four lanes met, and all Tacker could see was a signpost and the dim outline of a cluster of beech trees.

But he did not need the sign-post to tell him which way to take. He turned left and was at once going downhill again, seawards at first and then swinging in a big curve around the village.

He began to run, for no reason except that it was easy to be going down after the climb up. His feet made a muffled pad-pad on the worn stone road surface.

After a mile the lane brought him out on to the shore road. He paused at the gateway in which, two days earlier, he had sheltered to let the Wickham's car go past. So after all, he had come to a place where he was in easy reach of the Rifle House. He was about to turn away from the gate, impatient with himself, when a faint sound came out of the mist, and then a blurred moving figure. A moment later Sarah Wickham was standing in front of him. Her face, white in the fog, ran with tears.

'Please can you help – ?' she began, and then recognized Tacker and broke off.

But he had heard all he needed, and had one leg over the gate already.

'Come on – you'll have to hold him,' he shouted over his shoulder, and raced towards the sound.

The Corgi was in a trap beyond the far hedge. There were sheep-worn gaps in the hedge-top. Tacker climbed one of these and paused to look back. He saw the girl labouring along, bent forward, evidently hampered by a stitch in the side.

He went quietly to the trap, murmuring encouragement to the dog.

The Corgi squatted back on three legs, its right front paw caught between the blunt saw teeth, its thick chestnut coat and white chest blaze matted with earth. It panted and tugged as the rabbit had done, and every now and then gave a high-pitched cry.

Tacker began to pull off his old ragged sweater. He had worn it because of the fog-chill in the air; now it would be useful.

When Sarah joined him, he said, 'When I springs the trap, see he don't try to run off. He'll be wild-like, after being caught, and we'd lose him again in the mist.'

'He bit me just now,' she observed, in a tone of surprise rather than complaint.

He glanced at her hands and saw that there was blood on one of them from a gash around the thumb. Against his will he began to feel some regard for her. She was not fussing about the hurt.

'Beastly traps. Beastly cruel traps.' She began to cry a little again, and he had the impression that it was with anger against the trappers more than anything else.

'They're not meant for dogs,' he told her sententiously. 'Dogs shouldn't stray in the fields.'

'Rabbits or dogs, traps are cruel. And Budge wouldn't have strayed if someone hadn't left the gate open. He must have been here for hours. Ever since last night, probably.'

'Don't reckon he has.'

'Why not?'

But Tacker did not mean to let her know that he had searched for the dog the previous evening, and would have heard it from the shore road if it had been in the trap then. He handed Sarah his sweater. 'Hold him with this and mind your fingers or you'll get another bite.'

She watched as Tacker gently moved the gin to get at its release spring. The dog snarled repeatedly and snapped helplessly at the trap and his helpers. Sarah talked to him all the time and grasped him around the shoulders and body, her hands protected by the layers of wool.

Tacker pressed the spring with his foot. The dog struggled and yelped but the steel jaws did not move. The boy trod down with all his force; the trap yielded, but not enough. Sweating a little, Tacker changed feet and tried again, and

suddenly the dog's paw was free, and Sarah was trying to stop him from leaping away recklessly on three legs. She hugged him as he began to quieten and murmured again and again 'Thank goodness. Oh, thank goodness.'

'Shall I take him?' Tacker offered.

'Better not. He knows me. I must get him home quickly. 'But – ' she looked at Tacker uncertainly ' – could you come with me? It'll be difficult, going over hedges or through gates.'

'I'll do the gates. Come on. There's a lane not far off. We'll go down that.'

The lane ran straight across Mr Veale's land. Ordinarily Tacker avoided it, for fear of coming upon Mr Veale unexpectedly round a sharp bend. But today he was prepared to risk it. He was, after all, on an innocent errand, even though

Mr Veale might disagree, judging that, first, the dog should not have been on his land and, second, had sprung a trap meant for a rabbit, which would now need to be reset.

Tacker led the way to a gate in the bottom corner of the field and pushed it open with a swagger of gallantry. The lane plunged downhill between high banks that arched overhead: today its summer greenness was a tunnel of fog.

The dog was calmer. He lay limp, exhausted by pain and fear, the damaged, swollen paw dangling.

Presently Sarah was forced to stop and lean against a bank, one knee raised to take the weight that seemed to her to grow with every yard of the rough ground.

'Thank you for doing the trap,' she said, after resting a minute. 'I wasn't going to ask you. I didn't think you'd help me after what you said the other day.'

Tacker went dull red. He did not want to be thanked, but he did not want to be accused of heartlessness either. And he certainly did not want to talk about his behaviour the previous Sunday.

'You'd best ways learn to spring a trap,' he countered. 'Visitors' dogs are always getting caught. Cats, too.'

'We're not visitors,' Sarah reminded him as she hefted the Corgi higher in her arms and set off again. 'We're living here now. Why did you say all that, the other evening?'

'Can't explain now,' Tacker muttered, and she let it go; carrying the dog left her too little breath for talk.

In the short time they were in the leafy tunnel, the mist thinned and grew luminous. Gradually the sun was striking down to the hidden land. Strands of vapour parted, showing the sky. Trees, walls and hedges began to stand out again.

When they reached the Rifle House gate, Tacker opened it for Sarah and shut it again behind her, remaining on the outside.

She looked round in surprise. 'Come on,' she said. 'Come in and see my mother and father. And I've got your jersey. Though it'll have to be washed. It's got earth and blood on it.'

At that moment the door opened behind her and Mrs Venn stood there, mop poised to be shaken out. She paused, motionless, and stared from one child to the other.

For an instant Tacker stared back at her; then whirled about and ran off into the brightening mist.

Six

At the Sailor's Grave

Quickly, wonderfully quickly once it had begun to move, the last of the fog vanished away. The whole countryside was like an island rising undamaged from the sea. Every surface was wet, and sparkled in the returned sun.

Tacker sat on a gate and wondered what to do. He wished he had asked Sarah whether she had told her parents of his encounter with her in the stream. If so, would any gratitude they might feel for his help in the rescue of the dog offset their annoyance at his trespassing?

By this time they would know from his mother who he was. He could see that running away from a meeting with them had been a bit daft. As much as anything, a lingering feeling of guilt about the spell on the straw doll had made him do it.

He went home and took one of his remaining Woodbines from his wall-safe in the roofless outhouse.

The owl was not in the barn. Perhaps it had roosted in a tree, misled into thinking the extended twilight would soon turn to night again. Or perhaps it had another barn it went to when the mood took it.

Tacker climbed the ladder to the barn-loft. At the far end was a small window. He pushed it open, sat on the floor and lighted his cigarette. He puffed the smoke out of the window. As far as he knew, his mother had never come to look for him up here, but one could never be too careful.

The church clock chimed eleven. In less than an hour his mother would be back. He would feel stupid, facing her after running away. He couldn't think what to say – although that wouldn't matter very much, since in such situations she could always be relied on to say enough for both of them.

'Mazed!' Mrs Venn said. 'So mazed as a brish. What be *'bout*, Tacker? Running off up the road like a lamp lighter. I was proper ashamed.'

She had been going on in this strain for some time, and she went on a bit longer. Tacker, as he had anticipated, found nothing to say, but she would on the whole have been surprised if he had; she was used to his becoming mumchance after behaving in some unaccountable way.

From all her remarks, Tacker was able to gather one comforting fact; neither Sarah nor her parents had made any mention of his invasion of the Rifle House reach of the stream on Sunday.

'You're not so shy as all that, I'm sure,' Mrs Venn finished. 'Well, I suppose it's something that you helped to get the little dog out of the trap.'

She went into the kitchen to set about cooking the midday meal, and Tacker, released, rushed out to join whatever street games might be going at the moment.

That afternoon he was waiting his turn to rumble down the hill in a soap-box on wheels that had been commandeered from its owner, a mere eight-year-old, by several boys of Tacker's age. They let the eight-year-old have a ride occasionally just to stop him going home to tell his mother.

Tacker was startled by the sudden appearance of *his* mother.

'Come along,' she said. 'Hurry now.'

'Come where?'

'Home.'

'What for? I aren't done nothing.'

'Who said you had? Come along.'

Her manner was pleased; it did not seem to him that he was in any sort of disgrace, but he could not understand what she was being so secretive about.

As they drew near Bray Cottage she said 'There's a visitor for you. And don't you forget there's such a word as thank you.'

She opened the door of the parlour. Tacker halted abruptly. Sarah stood by the window. On the table lay a parcel.

'I'll just make a cup of tea,' said Mrs Venn, pushing Tacker forward and withdrawing.

Sarah stared at him thoughtfully. She knew more about him now. She liked to talk to Mrs Venn as she worked, in spite of her mother's attempts to discourage this. This morning, while her parents took Budge in the Trojan to the vet in Barlingford, she had questioned Mrs Venn about Tacker, taking care not to let her know that she had spoken to him before that morning. And so, indirectly, she had learned why Tacker resented newcomers at the Rifle House, as well as a good many details of his sayings and doings since babyhood, which interested her less.

'Hallo, Tacker,' she said. 'Why did you run away?' She had been disappointed that this was something Mrs Venn was unable to explain.

He ignored the question, since he could not answer it any better for her than he could for his mother.

'How's the little dog?' he asked.

'He'll be all right. He'll never be any use for show again, though. He'll just have to be a stud dog. He's asleep now. He's awfully tired!'

She took the parcel from the table and held it out to Tacker. He came forward slowly.

'This is for you. My mother and father asked me to thank you for helping Budge,' she said a little stiffly.

He muttered thanks and stood gazing down at the wrapping paper on which his name was written, as though a parcel were something new in his experience.

Mrs Venn came back into the room with a tray.

'Well, there now, what's this? Open it then, Tacker. He's been going on as though he's not quite 'zackly, lately,' she added aside to Sarah.

Tacker opened the parcel. Inside, lying in tissue paper in a shallow box, were a new dark blue pullover ('That's because we made such a mess of yours,' Sarah pointed out) and a paler blue shirt. In one corner was what looked like a fat bundle of tissue paper. It was heavy, and Tacker unrolled strip after strip of paper from it, to reveal at last a big clasp knife with a selection of assorted implements in addition to two blades.

Tacker was inarticulate with surprise and pleasure, his mother voluble. She made him go away to wash and change into the shirt and pullover, and his best shorts, before joining Sarah and herself for tea.

He took his time. Once upstairs, he sat in the sun on the low sill of the long corridor window and examined all the gadgets on the knife at leisure.

He remembered carving the shrunken head and wishing for a better knife. He had not expected the wish to come true at all; to find it come true through the Wickhams made him

feel almost uneasy. He knew he would think twice before indulging in spells again. Another time they might turn out less well – both for him and whoever else was involved.

After tea Sarah said she must go over to the Rectory; she was due for a piano lesson from the Rector's daughter.

'Will you be able to play, then, with that bite you had from the little dog?' Mrs Venn asked.

Sarah looked at the base of her thumb, where a strip of sticking plaster covered an area of skin stained brown with iodine.

'It's a bit stiff, but not enough to get me out of a lesson,' she said.

To Tacker Mrs Venn said, 'You can step across as far as the Rectory gate with Miss Sarah. And on the way back, go and show Granfer your new things. I saw him working around the south side of the church not long since.'

Tacker turned on his mother an appalled and unbelieving face. She couldn't mean to send him out, all dressed up, on a weekday afternoon – and with this girl too. Anyone might see him. The teasing would never stop. And to crown all, it would get about that he had gone looking for the Wickhams' dog. The other boys would think him soft.

'Hadn't I best change first?' he suggested desperately. 'I might get these things mucked up.'

'Change? Just to walk through the churchyard? Anyhow, you can't show Granfer your new shirt and that if you haven't got them on, can you?'

Defeated, he hung back while Sarah and his mother said their good-byes, and then fairly bolted across the road to the lych gate. His mother called after him in reproof.

When Sarah caught up with him she said, 'What's the

matter? Don't you like being dressed up? Will the other boys tease you?'

' 'Course not,' he said, startled by her perception.

'I don't like being too tidy,' she went on. 'In the garden I wear the oldest things I can. My mother says I look as though I belonged to the gipsies.'

They reached the wooden bridge across the stream, which divided the old churchyard from a hillside where in recent years Tacker's grandfather had dug new graves.

Sarah paused and looked down into the water. 'This is the same stream, isn't it? The one that goes through our garden? I've built some more of that path along it. Come down and see it one day, if you're not angry about it any more.'

'All right,' he said, without believing that she meant the invitation seriously.

She went through the gate into the Rectory garden and across the wide gravel sweep to the house.

Through one of the tall windows Tacker could see the sombre cassocked figure of the Rector pacing to and fro, composing his sermon, perhaps.

Inside his head Tacker mimicked the Rector's pulpit voice, opening and shutting his mouth soundlessly.

'Now-a my fr-r-en-des, we come to this thot. It is better for us hee-ar in this sorry world to think each day that we may . . .' May what? What did the Rector go on about in that chopped-up way of his, as though his words were little bits of carrot in a grater?

For Tacker, Molly's departure to work in Barlingford had meant one blessed freedom: no one bothered to tidy and clean him up every Sunday and take him off to church, as she had done because she enjoyed the service.

Tacker had not enjoyed it; it had been to him a dreadful

oppression of spirit, especially on fine days of spring and summer. He was thankful that, once Molly had left, his mother had not insisted that he should go to church.

He leaned over the split-pine handrail of the bridge. Drops of amber resin oozed out of the knots. He picked some off and rubbed them between his fingers to get the pine smell.

From the Rectory came the sound of careful scales on the piano. Tacker poised his hands over the rail in grotesque imitation of Miss Wilkinson, at school, about to play a march on the twanging piano. He cocked up his knuckles and ran his fingers awkwardly up and down.

Two girls at the village school took piano lessons at the Rectory. Both were considered to 'fancy themselves'. Perhaps Sarah would join that group – if she went to the village school. But would she? Probably not, he thought. She would go to one of those odd schools that They went to, and had to pay for. So it was no use her pretending to be friendly with him, and say he could go down to the Rifle House. Of course he couldn't. Soon she would have lots of school friends, and not want to know him.

He felt somehow relieved at this decision. It was some weeks now since he had accepted the idea that the Great Green Gorge of the Orinoco would be forbidden territory from that time on. Suppose he were to take Sarah at her word, only to find that her parents disapproved? No, it was much better to ignore the whole thing.

He left the bridge and went slowly along the path towards the lych gate. He hadn't forgotten that his mother had told him to show his new clothes to his grandfather, but he doubted whether the old man was much interested in clothes. The ones he wore did not suggest it.

For some time, Tacker had felt an awkwardness in meeting his grandfather. Until the coming of Miss Lumley the old man had been his story-teller, adviser and confidant, the person he went to when he was at a loose end, or out of favour at home, or wanting an explanation of some new and bothering aspect of human behaviour.

Once it had seemed to him that his grandfather had roamed the whole world, and that his stories of his travels would never be exhausted. He had been a walker of Shire stallions, and had a quantity of anecdotes about the people and places he had seen.

Tacker's realization that the travels had been only across the counties of southern England, and that the anecdotes could be repeated until they lost their spell, coincided more or less with his first encounter with Miss Lumley. From then on he went less and less often to talk to the old man while he was at work, or visit him in his widower's tiny, untidy cottage.

And the old man, meeting his grandson in the street, had not omitted a wry comment, so that the boy had been reduced to mumbling excuses.

At the corner of the church Tacker was halted by the sound of voices on the hill outside Bray Cottage. His gang was playing there. If he ran the gauntlet in his new clothes it would mean questions, a scuffle, perhaps a proper fight – right outside his own home too.

He turned aside, and threaded a way among the grave stones to the farthest corner of the south side of the churchyard. Here he had a wall at his back and fuchsia bushes hid him from the road eight feet below. Near the wall was a late eighteenth century grave, a mere hump in the grass with a slate slab for a headstone. Tacker knew it as the Sailor's Grave, and it had long been one of his refuges.

The inscription on the slate slab, barely legible now,

said: 'John Hobson, seaman, of H.M. Brig-of-War *Kestrel*. Lost off Whittenhoe, 3 March 1797.'

Tacker had first had the inscription read to him and the story of the wreck told him by his grandfather when he was a very small boy. From time to time he had begged to hear it again.

'Terrible thing it was, terrible,' the old man would say. 'Ship of war lost like that on the rocks, every man aboard drowned. Ay, and a woman, too, d'you know that? A woman, that nobody didn't never know how she got herself there. But her body came in on Combascott beach, same tide as a dozen or more of the poor sailors. Bodies was coming in on all the beaches around the coast for weeks after that wreck. There's some buried in parishes all along. Just one man of the *Kestrel* lived to tell the tale, and he never sailed out of Abbotstowe.'

'Why not?' Tacker would ask.

'Too sick, likely. Or changed places with that there foolish woman, some said.'

'Gave her his clothes to dress up in?'

'Might have done.'

'What happened to him afterwards?'

'Never heard. Went off to join some other ship, probably.'

'Go on about the wreck,' Tacker would say.

'Wreck? Well, I told you.'

'Not all of it.'

'Keep interrupting, you do. There's nothing to tell. She went on the rocks.'

'Yes, but before that. Why was she in a little place like Abbotstowe?'

'She'd put in for repairs after a storm. Funny, that, isn't it? Weeks she was, being put right, and then away she goes into another storm and it's good-bye for ever. Terrible thing it was,' the old man would repeat, and pause and sigh for the long-ago sorrow of the sea. 'And it shouldn't never have happened. Abbotstowe men warned the captain not to sail on that tide. They knew the storm was coming. But he wouldn't listen.'

'Why not?'

'Why not? Why not? Becausc hc was a proud Navy captain and they was ignorant fishermen that couldn't read or write. But he sailed out of the Barling river a dead man, and a hundred dead men with him. Up anchor and away she went, the *Kestrel*, bound for Portsmouth. The storm must have met her out in the Channel not two hours later. She beat back in the darkness, driven up north-east, and couldn't reach the Barling mouth, seemingly. The south-westerly wind would still be driving her, though she wouldn't have a stitch of canvas on her by that time. And Whittenhoe was waiting for her. Must have been somewhere around one or two o'clock in the morning, in the black dark, that she crashed on the Kestrel Rock and split abroad. It wasn't called the Kestrel Rock then, of course – that's only since.'

At this point he would usually fall silent for some while, musing as though the wreck had happened in his lifetime, and he was seeing in his mind's eye remembered scenes. Finally prompted by his listener, he would go on, 'The wreckage had to be picked up, off the beaches and off the rocks – it was Admiralty business to see that everything was saved that could be, and sold for what it would fetch. *My* grandfather was one of those that helped in that work.'

'What sort of stuff was it?' Tacker would ask, even after he had heard it a dozen times.

'All sorts. Hammocks, blankets, cable, tarpaulins, copper

sheet and iron and lead. And sails, and the masts. A retired captain that lived here in Hamblecombe bought the mainmast. Put it up in his garden for a flagpole.'

As the story came to its end, Tacker would regret that there had been no splendid shipwreck on Whittenhoe in his lifetime, no great dramatic loss, no salvaging of wreckage from the rocks and beach.

In the early years after he first heard of the *Kestrel*, his daytime self dreamed of daring rescues of drowning seamen; at night drowned seamen, green as weed and cold as fear, trailed dripping through the churchyard, hunting him. Or John Hobson's sea-filled eyes would glare through the bottle-glass pane of his window and scream with the voice of the wind.

Yet he still asked his grandfather, now and again, to tell him the story of the *Kestrel*. And still came, in warm calm weather, to lie on the scythe-shaved grass by John Hobson's grave, as he had today.

Below in the road he heard his usual companions scuffle and shout, and wished they would go and do it somewhere else, so that he could run home and make himself respectably shabby again, and join them.

Abruptly part of his wish was granted. A boy came hurtling down the hill on a bicycle belonging to his elder brother, which he had borrowed in the brother's absence. At this time a bicycle was still a comparative rarity among the younger village boys, so the cyclist was at once pursued by the whole group with cries of 'Hey, Georgie Hancock! Giss a ride, Georgie! Giss a ride!'

In fifteen seconds the road was empty. Thankfully Tacker scrambled to his feet – only to duck back quickly into the shelter of the headstones. Round the corner of the church appeared Sarah and his grandfather.

He didn't want to meet Sarah in the company of his grandfather. He didn't want to meet her again today anyway. He had said his thankyous and good-byes, and that was that. He peered cautiously between the stones at ground level, watching them.

As they came into earshot he was startled to hear Sarah say '... and he's called Tacker Venn. Do you know him?'

'I know him,' the old man said, and looked straight at Tacker's hiding-place. 'Terrible young feller. You don't want to have much to do with a boy like that. Don't reckon your father and mother want you to go mixing with they rough village boys anyhow, do 'em?'

Sarah glanced at him, taken aback by the unfairness of this last question.

'They don't – ' she began, and then decided that the question didn't deserve an answer.

'I must be going now, otherwise they'll wonder where I am,' she said. 'Good-bye.'

The old man grinned to himself as he watched her go.

Tacker sat up. Had his grandfather seen him when he jumped to his feet just now, and had he called him a terrible young feller on purpose for him to overhear?

The old man came slowly to where Tacker sat. They regarded one another.

'What the 'Amlet are you doing hid away there, boy, dressed up fit to call on King George? Specially when there's a nice young leddy interested in you. You'll be walking out next.'

Ordinarily Tacker minded his grandfather's teasing less than that of any other adult, but this was going too far. Indignantly he stood up, ready to protest.

But his grandfather turned away, saying with a touch of bitterness, ‘No wonder I don’t see much of you any more. ’Tis only Rifle House friends that’ll do for you these days.’

Seven

The Owl in the Barn

To be accused by his own grandfather of getting above himself, or trying to, made Tacker so angry that he at once resolved never to go near the Rifle House again.

In any case, he told himself, his grandfather had got it all wrong. Of course he had gone to the Rifle House a lot in Miss Lumley's day. He had *worked* there. So had his mother, and she still did, and he didn't suppose *she* was told that nothing would do for her but Rifle House friends. As for Sarah, his meetings with her had been accidental. He had not tried to make friends with her, nor would he. The memory of the invitation to help build a path along the stream tugged at him. Yes, he'd like to go down to do that. But he wouldn't.

The days of a hot August ran on, broken sometimes by thunder. In the fields around the village, oats whitened to ripeness and the prawn-whiskered barley turned golden-bronze.

One morning, soon after breakfast, Tacker set out for a farm on the hillside to the east of Hamblecombe. His cousin Archie's father worked there. Archie had told Tacker that they would be cutting their oats that day, and he could come and help.

Turning a corner, he saw Sarah sitting on a low wall, eating a biscuit. A bicycle leaned beside her. A bicycle! How he longed to own one! How could he be friends with a girl who had a bicycle?

She said 'Hallo, Tacker. Have a biscuit?'

He declined a biscuit.

'I suppose you've had your breakfast,' she said. 'I haven't. Ours is always so late – nine or half past. Any old time. I get bored with waiting. Sometimes I take some biscuits and cheese and come out. Do you have yours early?'

'About seven o'clock.'

'I wish we did. In summer, anyway. Even eight would do. You're lucky.'

The idea that she should envy him anything, especially so humdrum a thing as early breakfast, struck Tacker as very odd.

'I'll have meals at regular times at school, anyway,' she observed, half to herself.

'You going away to school?' Tacker seized the chance to verify this.

'Not far. Only to Hillacombe. But I'll have to be a weekly boarder. I'd never get there in time in the morning by bus. I'll go in the car on Monday mornings and come back on Friday afternoons.'

Tacker thought about going away to school and felt thankful he didn't have to.

Sarah was looking at a small dark wooden door set at an angle in the wall on the other side of the road.

'What's that?' she asked getting down and going over to it.

Tacker opened the door for her to see. Inside was a little well, like a grotto in a cupboard, a shadowy place of moss and water drips. The well was in fact only a few feet deep, and perpetually brimmed with water, which trickled over its stone lip and ran away into the ditch below. It was fed by a spring in the bank behind it, twin to the source of the valley stream.

'Have you ever walked all along the stream, from here down to the sea?' Sarah asked.

Tacker considered. Had he? He supposed he hadn't – certainly not all at one time, although there were few stretches he hadn't explored. The stream had become familiar to him, piece by piece, year by year, until he knew most of its course as well as he knew the garden of Bray Cottage.

But he did not explain all this. He answered Sarah's question with a flat 'No.'

'Haven't you?' she stared at him. 'Why not? You live here.'

He was reminded of Miss Lumley's indignation when he told her he did not know where the stream rose. Rifle House friends indeed. He turned away.

'I knows the stream,' he said. 'All of it.'

'I was going to ask you if you'd come with me to explore it today. But you wouldn't, would you? You've never even come down to help build the path.'

Tacker felt some compunction, and did not know how to show it. 'I'm off harvesting,' he said by way of apology.

'Harvesting!' Her eyes brightened. 'I wish I – but I suppose they wouldn't let me.'

Who did she mean by *they*, he wondered. Her parents? The farmers?

She pulled her bicycle away from the wall. 'Well, goodbye, Tacker. I must go home and have breakfast.'

She pedalled away. Tacker walked on. Beyond the well in its cupboard, the road curved. He glanced back, and at the same instant Sarah turned. She waved, and Tacker, dimly aware that he had seemed surly, waved back with vigour.

The reaping machines travelled clattering around the fields, and the boys who stacked the sheaves in their wake became corn Arabs burned dark brown among the tented encampments of stooks. For their work they received only a few pence and a midday meal of bread and cheese and cider, but they did not care.

For the first few days of harvest Tacker was content to go to bed an hour or more before his usual time. Mrs Venn smiled to herself and gave him purified goose fat, the time-honoured country remedy, to rub on his burning, scratched, and blistered arms and hands, and for once he accepted the attention without accusing her of fussing.

When the village school reopened, Miss Wilkinson was faced with a roomful of exuberant, dark-skinned barbarians who wanted less than ever to be shut away indoors at desks.

One afternoon in September, with three days to go before her own term began, Sarah went to Bray Cottage with a message from her mother. Usually Mrs Venn worked at the Rifle House on Saturday mornings, but on this Saturday the Wickhams intended to drive over to visit a Corgi kennels some fifty miles away, to see a brood bitch the owner had for sale.

Mrs Venn invited her into the little sitting-room, where she was ironing. The room was full of the smell of warm clean linen dried in the open air.

'Now what about Monday?' Mrs Venn asked. 'I couldn't manage the morning, you see, because that's my own wash-day. But if it would suit, I could come around two o'clock.'

Sarah said it would suit; she had been told to accept Monday afternoon if it was offered. She watched as Mrs Venn took a flat iron from the oil stove, held it against her cheek to test it, and put it back again with a 'tch' of annoyance.

' 'Tis so slow, the old stove. In winter, when I have my range burning, they irons heat up lovely. But the weather's too hot for it now.'

'I'd never seen anyone ironing with flat irons until we came here.'

'No, well, in thc town where you were, you had the electric, didn't you? Perhaps one day they'll bring us the electric out here. Your mother'd be glad – she doesn't care for these, I know. But I've never used nothing else. I don't mind them, especially when I've got the range to heat them, change and change about, nice and quick. In summer we only light it up on Sundays, for the roasting and bread baking and that.'

'Do you make all your own bread?'

'Always have done. My mother taught me.'

She stood a moment gazing out at blood-drop fuchsia flowers hanging in sunlight against the churchyard wall.

'I can see our old farmhouse kitchen as clear as clear,' she said. 'My mother used to send a bushel of our wheat to the mill every week, and from the flour she'd make fourteen loaves.'

'Where was the mill?' Sarah asked, puzzled. She was thinking of pictures she had seen of old mills in other parts of the country, holding their great sails to the sky. She had noticed nothing like that in the villages.

'Why, it was in Combascott, the top end, where the road goes up sharp. The house there is still called Mill Cottage. There used to be a dam, and a water-wheel to drive the mill.'

Of course, a *water* mill, Sarah thought. A water-wheel – she could remember once being taken to see one turning: a smooth curve of water falling from the lip of an old wooden sluice into the vanes of the wheel, pushing them down one after the other, so that the wheel plodded heavily round, flinging plumes of drips from its sides. Once the valley stream had worked a wheel like that, serving the villages by grinding the corn for their bread. She wished it did still.

'Would you like to take home some apples for your mother?' Mrs Venn asked. 'We've got more than we can do with. If you don't mind picking them yourself, I'll give you a basket, and then if you'll excuse me, I'll go on with this old ironing. I must finish before Mr Venn gets home. If Tacker was in from school I'd ask him to pick some apples for you, but he plays around in the street so long, I never know when he'll be back.'

This was the first time Sarah had been into the garden of Bray Cottage. The sight of the big barn surprised her.

She went to the doorway and took a few steps into the dimness.

There came a sudden movement in the far corner, and a silent gliding rush of pale wings. She flinched and closed her eyes; then realized what it was and ran out eagerly to gaze up. The owl rose in moth-soft flight and was gone over the roofs. If only she had known it was there! If only she could have watched it without disturbing it!

And then she became aware that someone was watching *her*, and turned to see Tacker at the back door.

'That's my owl,' he said as he came towards her.

To this, a village child would automatically have said, 'Git 'oom,' meaning, 'Get on with you.'

But Sarah took it for granted that he was speaking the truth.

'Is it? How did you tame it? Did you find it when it was young? I wish I hadn't frightened it away.'

'He don't like strangers. He'll come to me,' Tacker said, astonished at being believed, and carried away by his old fantasy of owl-owning. At the same time he found himself regarding her with subdued admiration. From her manner, it was evident that she had not felt the panic that always filled him when the bird flew out from its perch. He suspected that she might indeed be capable of taming it. He remembered how she had ignored the pain in her hand when the trapped Corgi bit her. She wasn't soft, that was sure.

He did not want to be questioned too closely on methods of owl taming – but he did want to demonstrate his own skill and courage in some way. Nothing presented itself except climbing apple trees.

He held out his hand for the basket.

'Come on,' he said, 'I'll pick you some apples.'

Eight

Downstream by Moonlight

Tacker leaned out of the window in the upstairs corridor of Bray Cottage and looked at the moonlit garden. It was the moonlight that had wakened him: a stone glare reflected into his bedroom from the churchyard wall. For a while he had tried to go to sleep again, but there was a mysterious excitement in the pale light outside. When the church clock chimed one, and he realized that everyone else in the village would have been in bed long since, he got up and put on his clothes.

Where should he go? Into the garden, to the roofless outhouse? Downstream, across Mr Veale's land? He had never made a foray by night over that territory. And beyond that, why shouldn't he discover what the Great Green Gorge of the Orinoco looked like on a night like this?

Silently he went downstairs and opened the back door, that was never locked. The entrance to the barn was a dark mouth to be skipped past quickly. He had never feared the outdoor night, whether under moonlight, starlight, or thick cloud; only the indoor dark held bogies.

From the grass plot he gazed about him. Slate roofs gleamed steely under the moon. Angles were sharp with shadow. Lime-washed walls gave back the moon's whiteness.

He looked up. High and solitary, in pale lucent blue, spun the great straw-gold moon of harvest.

He left the garden by a gap in the hedge and crossed the vegetable plot of another cottage to reach the stream. He took off his plimsolls and stepped in. Two hundred yards of wading past back gardens brought him out into the fields. He wiped cold feet on the grassy bank, put on his shoes and sat where he was for a while, looking back at the silent, moonlit village.

Once more he was the scout for an attacking party. He could carry word that the white settlers lay at their mercy.

In the still September air two sounds were astonishingly loud: the rasping of field crickets and the rilling voice of the stream. Suddenly the cry of an owl broke in and Tacker wondered if it was *his* owl. But no, of course, it was the signal: the signal from his tribe, waiting for his message. He must go on.

The rickyard of the farm was full of new stacks. Over them a bat flickered like a piece of burnt paper in a draught. Here was the tribe's village of pole and leaf-thatch huts; here the scout delivered his message to the chief.

And having done so, changed roles, to become the witch doctor again. It would be fitting for him to call upon the gods of the river forests, from the depths of the Great Green Gorge, to grant success to the raid.

In skirting the farm buildings he kept well away from the yard where the chained sheepdog lay in its kennel. In the little meadow below the Rifle House, light filtered through the alder leaves and flecked the rippled water.

Tacker ducked under the blackthorn barrier into a pool of brightness, but ahead lay the Gorge itself, deep in shadow; the sight of it made him pause. But he soon saw that the Gorge, full of blackness at first sight, was in fact splashed with light that fell through gaps between elm and hawthorn, hazel and ash. He waded forward once more, and turned aside for a moment to climb the steps Miss Lumley had cut to her dipping place. The back of the Rifle House lay in shadow, its windows dark, and below it stood the new kennels with their surrounding runs. He knew from his mother that the Wickhams now owned about a dozen dogs.

Some way up the Gorge he noticed a change in the bank on the Rifle House side. Some of it had been sheared away, and earth and stones had been built up to make a path, perhaps eighteen inches wide and two inches above the level of the water. Stooping, he waded alongside, examining the path in the faint, silvery light.

When he straightened up something harsh and rustling touched him on the back of the head. He made a startled sound in his throat and gooseflesh burst out on his arms and shoulders. As he swung round to face whatever it was he tripped, and splashed about before he could recover his balance.

Suspended from a twig-stump by a cord tied around its waist, a straw doll swayed gently from its contact with him. He stared at it; his heart still thudded from the fright it had given him. Then he peered more closely. Was it the one he had made and sent sailing downstream? It looked bigger, yet the body was tied together as he had tied it. But it had plaited straw hair now, a cork face marked with eyes and nose, and a straw skirt decorated with scraps of cloth and bits of wood.

He grinned at it. It *was* his, and Sarah had found it, and taken the trouble to improve on his handiwork – though of course she could not have known who had made it. He groped in his pockets for something to add to its finery. All he could find was a bit of string. He bound this two or three times around the doll, knotted it and fluffed out the ends into tassels. There. What would Sarah make of that? Would it puzzle her?

While he was adorning the doll he became aware of sounds from the kennels. The noise he had made when the doll startled him had evidently disturbed one of the dogs; it began to give a series of muttering, sleepy growls. Suddenly this dog, or another, uttered a long-drawn howl, and was instantly answered by two or three others. In ten seconds all the dogs were howling in unison.

Shocking because unexpected, Mr Wickham's voice broke in on the hubbub. 'Be quiet, will you!' he shouted from one of the Rifle House windows. The howl wavered, but picked up again. Mr Wickham muttered something. Tacker listened intently. Was he coming out to the kennels? The answer was soon given by the crunch of footsteps on the path alongside the runs. Tacker guessed that Mr Wickham had come down the quick way, through the trap door into the cellar.

Mr Wickham rapped on the wooden walls of the kennels and shouted again, 'Be quiet, all of you!'

At this, Mrs Wickham's voice called from the window, 'What is it, Edward?'

'Kennel howl. Didn't you hear them? The moon, probably, but I just wanted to make sure there wasn't anything else about to disturb them.'

The dogs had fallen silent. Tacker looked towards the Great Falls. Dimly he could make out the dark line of Sarah's path running upstream, from where he stood to the foot of the falls. It seemed to be time he went. He began to put on his plimsolls again. The wet canvas did not feel pleasant against his feet as it did on hot summer days; only clammy and cold. He began to wish it wasn't so far to walk home, and wondered what time it was. He felt sure he would sleep all right now, once he got back to bed.

Very softly he walked to the falls, and emerged into moonlight, which glinted on the glassy curve at the lip of the fall, and shone on the white swirling pool below.

Dreamy with fatigue, he watched the hypnotic water, lulled by its soft roar. He forgot the Wickhams, the dogs; forgot being a witch-doctor; and when after a while he moved on to climb the bank beside the fall, forgot caution.

From the Rifle House came a little cry, answered by Mr Wickham calling 'What's wrong, Alice? What's happened?'

Tacker leapt down on to the pulpy straw of the rickyard and ran into the alley between the stacks. He crouched and listened.

Mrs Wickham was saying, 'I saw something by the stream. It went through the hedge.'

'What sort of thing?'

'I'm not sure. I only saw it out of the corner of my eye.'

'Farm dog, perhaps.'

'No. It was bigger than that.'

'Stray sheep, d'you think?'

'I don't think so. No, it couldn't have been, it moved too fast. I thought – I must have been imagining things, but I thought it was a boy.'

'*Boy*? At this time of night?'

Tacker heard Mr Wickham striding up and down the boundary hedge. He poked into the nettles and leafy elm underbrush with a stick, and called sharply 'Anyone there? Anyone there?'

Tacker kept very still.

Finally Mr Wickham said, 'Can't see anything. Whatever

it was, it's gone. I think you imagined the boy. More likely a village dog straying around for scraps.'

Footsteps went back towards the house, and Tacker made his way between the warm walls of straw to the far end of the rickyard. Here he came on a hay stack, its upper half sliced away on one side, leaving a shelf at about waist height from the ground. He gazed at it longingly. He was very tired.

The open side of the stack was out of sight of the farm lane. If he slept in the hay, he would wake when the sun rose – and even if he wasn't home before his mother was up, it wouldn't matter. He would pretend he had got up early and gone out, a thing he did often enough in fine weather.

On the rail of the cart that rested on its shafts in the shed at the side of the yard hung an empty sack. He took this and climbed on to the hay shelf. When he had burrowed himself a comfortable hollow in the summer-smelling hay, he spread the sack over his back and shoulders, and in three minutes was asleep.

And twelve miles away, in her bed at school, Sarah watched the moon through the high narrow windows of the mid-Victorian house in which the boarders slept. Its light on her face had awakened her. The other girls in the dormitory were asleep. She saw that her little travelling clock said twenty to three. It was Thursday morning. Tomorrow afternoon she would go home for the week-end. She wished it could be *this* afternoon.

It wasn't that she was homesick, exactly. For one thing, the Rifle House was too recent a home for her to feel any deep attachment to it. But it was only a few months since she had left the town she had always known, and her friends there, in and out of school, and it seemed to her at this

moment that from now on she would always be lonely.

She thought of Bray Cottage, and Mrs Venn ironing and talking of the old mill and its water-wheel; she remembered the quick silent flight of the owl from its roost in the barn, and Tacker showing off as he climbed among the apple boughs. He interested, puzzled, and attracted her. His showing-off was the nearest he had come to any sign of liking her. But they would never be friends. I haven't any friends now, she thought, and I won't have any, not at school, not at home, not for years. She felt tears slide out from the corners of her eyes. The moonlight wavered and glittered.

Presently, between half-opened lids, she saw the room in a silver dazzle, and began to experiment to catch the changing rays of light on her wet lashes. She thought of the look of moonlight on water, and wished she could see the stream at home. But tomorrow night she would hear it from her bedroom window. If it was fine, she would be able to look out and see the trees along the bank, and the farm orchard beyond, and the fields on the hill.

The path along the bank would be in shadow. On Saturday she would build some more of it. She would add to it every time she went home, and by the end of term it would be finished – by the end of next holidays, anyway. It would run from end to end of the Rifle House reach of the stream. Then she would cut little terraces in the bank, doll-size terraces to be planted with bluebells, polyanthus, daffodils, iris, for next spring. The whole streamside would be a garden; her own particular garden . . .

Nine

Bicycles, Bicycles!

One cold, quiet October day, Georgie Hancock rode through Hamblecombe on a bicycle. It was the one he had ridden on the afternoon Tacker had hidden among the graves in his new clothes. Outside the shop he stopped and, still sitting astride, let the boys who had run after him catch up.

'It's mine now,' he announced. 'Len's give it me.'

His hearers said, 'Gor, he aren't,' and, 'Got 'oom,' and 'What for?'

Georgie, grinning, leaned back in the worn saddle and enjoyed their envy and chagrin. He was the first of the gang to acquire a bicycle, and it was a triumph, and he meant to make the most of it. He did not mind their reluctance to believe him; he would have felt the same in their place.

In the countryside at this time, at the end of the nineteen-twenties, farmers who had given up the use of pony and trap drove to market in very old square high motor cars, and their labourers rode to work on very, very old upright bicycles. And boys in the villages all somehow learned to ride as soon as their legs were long enough to reach the pedals while straddling the cross-bar. They could not hope to own bicycles for some while after that, but they boasted among themselves about the bicycles they would own, and each spent a lot of time scheming to acquire one.

For most boys, the best hope of getting a bicycle early (that is to say before he became a wage-earner) was to have an elder brother who could discard his own third-or fourth-hand machine on buying a better one or, possibly, an old motor-cycle. Georgie's elder brother, Len, was nineteen. He had a job in a garage in Barlingford, and had been saving hard, because his employer had promised to let him have a reconditioned motor-cycle cheap. The previous evening he had ridden home on the motor-cycle. And so Georgie had the discarded bicycle, and was one up on every boy of his age in the valley villages.

That evening Tacker asked his mother if he could use some of the money he had earned from Miss Lumley to buy a bicycle.

'Not a new one,' he added hastily. 'Just a second-hand.'

'That money's in the Post Office Savings Bank and it can't be taken out. Leastways not unless it's for something urgent. And a bicycle's not urgent, I'm sure of that. You're not old enough yet. You'd be scarce tall enough to reach the pedals, sat in the saddle.'

'Ernie had a bike when he was the same age as me.'

'Ernie was tall for his age. Terrible old thing it was too.'

That was the trouble. If it hadn't been such a terrible old thing, Tacker thought, he might have been riding it all this summer past. Ernie had bought it from an older boy with a laboriously saved-up half-crown. It had been little more than a rusty frame on wheels, lacking mudguards, pump, lamp and handgrips. One day, not long before he left school, Ernie had been riding down the steep hill on which the stream rose. The defective brakes of his aged machine finally gave way, and after whirling faster and faster down the twisting road, he had seen a farm cart coming upwards and plunged into the hedge to avoid it. He had been bruised and cut; the bicycle had been buckled beyond repair.

Tacker went out into the garden. On the far side of the vegetable plot a tall hedge of runner bean plants shook and rustled. Overhead a south-westerly was shredding yellow-grey clouds to tatters, but it wasn't only the wind that swayed the bean rows. Alec Venn had picked the last pound or two of beans, and was beginning to strip the withering bines from their neat line of sticks.

His son's offer of help was accepted with a grunt, followed by 'Careful then. Don't go breaking the sticks. They'll do another year.'

Tacker had no great hopes of his father as an ally in the business of obtaining a bicycle, but he felt it might be worth mentioning.

'Georgie Hancock's got a bike,' he said.

'What's he want that for?'

This unpromising response was more or less what Tacker had expected and he decided to be blunt. 'I want one too.'

'Get away,' his father remarked amiably.

'I do,' Tacker insisted. 'Everyone's going to have one.'

'Who's everyone?'

'Archie and Walter and Sam and all those.'

'Ah, and go charging down hills breaking their legs, I dare say. You wait until you're a bit older, else you'll only do what Ernie did.'

Ernie, Ernie! Tacker tugged furiously at a bine and broke a stick.

'That'll do,' his father observed.

Tacker tried for a little longer to persuade him that he not only longed for but needed a bicycle, but his father refused even to argue about it, and presently Tacker fell silent.

Together they finished stripping the bean row, and piled the bines on the rubbish heap.

Alec Venn put a match to some twists of paper he had thrust under the wind-dried dead weeds. The flames fidgeted and crackled; the wind fanned them and they leapt up, flailing savagely this way and that.

Father and son watched, soothed by the pleasure of fire-making. They dodged the smoke that veered as though groping for them, and their hands and hair and clothes became lightly kippered.

It was growing dusk, and the air had a wintry feel. Soon it would be Guy Fawkes night, Tacker thought. It was time to start making a guy. He would suggest it to the others tomorrow. He had half a mind to make one of his own, and go round collecting pennies to be used, not for fireworks, but a bicycle fund. But he knew he wouldn't get many that way – and in any case it wasn't possible to be a lone wolf: the others would set on him and destroy his guy. Only communal efforts were approved in the village for things of that sort.

A few days later Ernie came home. The season was over, the paddle steamers laid up for the winter, but Ernie had managed to find himself a winter job in the docks at Cardiff. He announced this at tea on the evening of his arrival.

'Oh, Ernie – away over there?' his mother exclaimed. 'I was hoping you'd come back and find something round here. You'll hardly ever be home.'

At this, Ernie said something that startled them all. 'Nor I would be if I went away deep water. Nearly tried for a berth to Buenos Aires last week.'

'Oh no,' Mrs Venn said softly. She looked at him wonderingly. He was taller and broader than when he had gone away in the spring; his voice was deeper and he had adopted a sailor's swagger.

His mother's gaze moved to Tacker, who was staring at his brother in envy. Quickly she glanced down at her plate, because her eyes blurred with tears. Buenos Aires! All across the world! Wasn't that South America, the place Miss Lumley had known so much about? Tacker had told her little, directly, of the things Miss Lumley had spoken of to him, but she had gained a fair idea, both from occasional unthinking remarks of his, and from Miss Lumley herself. Was he full of dreams of jungles? Did he long to go off to see them for himself? If so, and Ernie *did* one day tire of his job in the docks and sign on some freighter bound for South America – and then came back talking of it . . .

Not many boys in the valley grew up with ambitions to be sailors, unlike those of the fishing villages only a few miles away. It had never occurred to Mrs Venn until this year that either of her sons might go to sea. She had been slightly disturbed when Ernie tried for the job on the paddle steamers, and got it, but she had comforted herself with the thought that it was a safe, inshore job, and seasonal; in the autumn he would come home and look for something near at hand. This talk of Buenos Aires frightened her.

And so when Ernie had gone back to Cardiff, Tacker found his mother unusually sympathetic and attentive. Not understanding the reason, and doubting it would last, he nevertheless set out to make the most of it, and began to talk eagerly of bicycles again. His mother, though still not enthusiastic, did not at once brush the subject aside this time.

She said, 'Well, one day, perhaps,' and, 'We'll see about it later.' When he became very insistent she said, 'Wait till your birthday, then.'

His birthday was in April, and it was barely November yet.

'All the others'll have bikes before then,' he protested.

But in spite of her fond and indulgent mood, Mrs Venn was not stirred by his urgency.

'Don't suppose they will,' she answered. And since he could not budge her from this, he went on trying to think of some way to get himself a bicycle as soon as possible, however old, and rackety, and lacking refinements.

In November another boy only a little older than Tacker had a birthday, and appeared in the street on a second-hand bicycle of quite presentable appearance. This sharpened the envy of all the others to a fierce edge, and they became quarrelsome. Tacker in particular began to make a name for himself as a fighter. On Saturdays, Tacker sometimes saw Sarah ride past on her bicycle, bound for music lessons at the Rectory, but they did not meet face to face, and she did not visit Bray Cottage again – nor he, the Rifle House.

Sarah herself gave all her out-of-school thoughts and energies to the building of her stream-side path, and by the beginning of the Christmas holidays it was finished – a narrow ledge of stones surfaced with beaten-down earth and weed-clods from the garden. The result was that this stretch of the stream was now narrower and slightly deeper than it had been. It flowed fast and strong, swollen by autumn rains; its level had risen, and so the path, after all her work, was only two or three inches above the water.

She put on Wellingtons and waded upstream, thinking of all the raking and digging and cutting away of the bank she had done. She wondered if Tacker had seen the finished path. She guessed that he came here secretly now and then, while she was at school; she had seen the string tassels he had tied around the straw doll, and felt sure that only he would have put them there.

Well, she had done it, without his help, and when the New Year came she would make the garden she had planned, along the bank.

She accepted now that, even if her parents had not been against it, there could be no friendships for her among the fierce-seeming groups of village children, who yelled and swore, and called mocking remarks after her as she rode past because she was a stranger and went to a different school; an odd-one-out who, by their standards, must be 'stuck-up'. It was true that Tacker had never shouted anything, but that, she thought angrily, was probably only because his mother worked for her parents, and he was afraid she might hear him.

Ten

A Visit from Miss Lumley

Tacker woke. It was midnight-dark, but he could hear his mother going downstairs, and knew it was morning. This was the mysterious time of year, when night came, friendly and domestic, into every ordinary morning; when to wake early was to hear cockcrow ring out from farm to farm around the village, and smell the sharp frost, and look out to see stars like splinters of ice.

He bundled out of bed and over the glassy linoleum to the window. The cold nipped his nostrils, but the warmth of sleep was round him like a cloak. He crouched at the sill. The glass was opaque with the lovely swirling patterns of fronds and sea-wrack, nature imitating itself, drawing pictures of itself, a thing Tacker always found puzzling. On one of the central panes the pattern was thin and blurred. He breathed on this and scraped a peep-hole with his fingernail. And there, outside, was the ghosty frost.

In the Atlantic coastal valleys, clear, bright frosts were common enough, but not this strange, white, quiet presence. He had seen it only once before, as a very small boy; and remembered it like a vision from an earlier life. He stared out in absorbed recognition.

The ghosty frost. Its sharp breath rasped his throat. Its pallor lightened the cock-crow dark. Thick rime whitened every surface and furred every twig. In the churchyard, old grey headstones glimmered in the haze, and marble stones stood out like blocks of snow.

There was a profound silence, and the whole height of the air was as still as a closed room.

Cold roused Tacker from his fascinated contemplation of the frost world. He hurled himself back into bed and wriggled down into the hollow of warmth still left. He rubbed his numb feet and then, without getting out again, began to dress. Faintly the smell of breakfast came up the stairs as his mother opened the back door to call 'Alec! Alec, it's time you were down.'

His clothes on him somehow, Tacker ran downstairs to the little warm haven of the kitchen, lit by a wavering candle flame and the mauve hissing glow of the primus. He shut the door behind him without needing to be told, and went slowly to the sink. He couldn't scamp washing, with his mother there, but he made it as swift a business as he could; there was always the excuse that he had to be finished before his father came down to shave. The well water was bitter cold.

He watched slices of bread frying in the dark iron pan. Although the range in the sitting-room was kept in, day and night, in weather as cold as this, it was low and sullen in the mornings; making it up doused its warmth still further. Therefore Mrs Venn cooked breakfast and brought the overnight kettle to the boil on the fast primus.

She lifted a half-piece of crisp fatty bread from the pan, drained it and put it on her chopping-board to cool, saying, 'There you are, then.'

Tacker burned his fingers and then his tongue in his eagerness to get the warm savoury food into his stomach and stave off the frost-sharpened pangs of morning hunger.

His father came in, shivering, and set about shaving, using a jug of hot water his wife had left ready on the draining-board.

Tacker sat on the kitchen chair and crunched his fried bread and stared at the endlessly fascinating and frightening task. (Alec Venn used a cut-throat razor.)

Mrs Venn said, 'Don't forget there's a visitor for tea today, Tacker.'

Her husband drew the blade away from his jaw abruptly, and turned to her a startled face, clownish with its lather mask.

'What visitor?' he asked in alarm.

'Oh, you needn't fret. She'll be gone, time you come home, I dare say. I'll get you your tea same as usual.'

'Who is it, then?'

'Miss Lumley. Didn't I tell you? Saw her yesterday, down the Rifle House. She's staying there a day or two.'

'Oh ah,' her husband said without interest, only relieved to know that his evening meal would not be ruined by polite chat.

Tacker thought about seeing Miss Lumley again. He had forgotten it was today she was coming; first the ghosty frost and then the longing for warmth and food, had put it out of his mind. His mother had come back from the Rifle House a few days earlier with the news that Mrs Wickham had had a letter from Miss Lumley, telling her of an unwanted present she had been given: a puppy of that rare breed, the Italian Greyhound.

'It was sent her by an old lady that breeds them,' Mrs Venn reported to her family. 'Miss Lumley's godmother, she is. But Miss Lumley says she can't do with a dog, so she asked Mrs Wickham if she could bring the puppy to them, and let them see it and help her decide what to do. They've asked her to stay a day or two with them.'

Miss Lumley had duly arrived at the Rifle House, and Mrs Venn had talked to her on her next working visit. Miss Lumley had said she would call at Bray Cottage before returning to Cornwall, upon which Mrs Venn had asked her to tea.

A tea party, Tacker thought. He would be made to wear his best shorts and socks, and the shirt the Wickhams had given him, with a long-sleeved pullover this time because it was so cold. He would have clean hands and face and well-combed hair, and altogether feel proper soft.

He wanted to see Miss Lumley again. He would have liked to talk to her alone, as he had in the old days – or listen while she talked. But here at home, under his mother's mind-your-manners eye – oh, no. He had half a mind to slip off after school and 'forget' to appear for tea.

Mrs Venn dished up the breakfast and gave Tacker his plate to carry into the lamp-lit sitting-room, where the range was just beginning to glow a little, and its night-long warmth hung in the room.

This morning there was a letter from Molly. Mrs Venn read it with an occasional frown or sniff. Molly's letters, and her manner on her visits home, had been growing more cheerful in recent months; she talked less of home-sickness and more of boy-friends. She had, it seemed, two. One was the grocer's boy, and the other a young plumber she had met at a dance to which she had gone with the parlourmaid of the house where she worked.

Mrs Venn didn't like the sound of either of them, but wanted to inspect them both. On the other hand, she didn't want Molly to take the definite step of bringing one of them home. Her uncertainty about all this was making her irritable.

In Tacker's eyes, Molly had improved. For one thing, on her occasional week-end visits home she brought him little presents out of her wages; for another, she no longer burst into tears when she had to leave to catch the bus back to Barlingford. But best of all, she had completely given up all attempts to make him go to church with her.

He ate bacon and fried bread with fierce appetite; went on, slowing down, to bread and butter and home-made rhubarb jam. Finally he drank his tea, and tried to catch his mother's eye. She made him wait two minutes; then gave him a nod. He slid off his chair and ran out to fetch his jacket and school boots.

Recently he had taken to going as far as the bus stop each weekday morning with his father, and so when Alec Venn stood up and said his ritual 'I'm off, then,' Tacker pulled on his jacket and followed him out into the white-rimed half-light and the strong, pure smell of frost.

The man clumped up-hill with the steady tread of a labourer. His studded boots crunched on the fine grit of the road. As usual Tacker longed to clump like that, but even in winter, wearing boots, the richness imparted by weight was missing.

Out of the dimness came the sound of another slow, slack-kneed tread, and Tacker's grandfather appeared, a long-handled spade over his shoulder, its shield-shaped blade wrapped in sacking. He looked like Father Time with the wrong implement.

He paused and regarded his son and grandson.

'Hallo, Da,' the younger man said. 'Starting on old Harry Dart's grave today? Ground'll be hard.'

'That's why I'm starting today. Never be dug come time for the funeral, else.'

Alec Venn made a move as though to go on his way. But he checked and turned back to say, 'Did you manage to see to that, what Annie talked to you about, Da?'

'Done a bit of it.'

'Well, not long to Christmas now, is it?'

'Don't you worrit, I'll see to it.'

Christmas? See to what, Tacker wondered as he walked

on beside his father. What were they talking about? But he knew it was useless to ask.

When they rounded the corner by the Queen's Head they saw the lights of the green single-decker shining from its stop by the General (A. Luxton) Stores. But Alec Venn did not hurry his step. He knew that the conductor would not ring his bell until he was aboard.

He gave Tacker a sideways nod in farewell and climbed the steps to join other first-bus regulars. Tacker ran ahead. He had to reach the forge before the bus. It was his newest craze. Every morning he raced down the street from the Stores to the forge as though a demon were after him. He heard the engine rumble into life; the bus began to roll forward and its headlights washed the cottage walls with yellow light.

Heart thudding, Tacker jumped to sanctuary – the lowest step of the blacksmith's cottage – as the bus roared past. He waved, and his father waved back.

As he wandered home he puzzled over the snatch of talk between his father and grandfather. Should he visit his grandfather and try to find out what it was he had said he'd see to? Or would that only make the old man start talking about Rifle House friends again? Not that he had any reason to, now. Except that Miss Lumley was coming to tea.

Not long to Christmas. School closed next week. Midwinter frost, and Christmas coming, and holidays, and secrets, and shouting carols in the street and knocking for pennies, and his mother stirring great dark bowlsful of pudding mixture.... Suddenly his chest swelled with joy. He broke into a run again, and added his white breath to the foggy pallor of the air as he galloped home to warm himself by the range before school.

That afternoon Tacker sat opposite Miss Lumley at the

tea table, and cast a covert glance at her now and again in the lamplight, as she talked to his mother. She had asked especially, when accepting Mrs Venn's invitation, that they should have tea in the sitting-room. Mrs Venn was not altogether happy about it; she felt uneasily that, even though it was by her visitor's own request, she was not really 'doing her proud'. Left to herself, she would have lighted the fire in the icy, low-ceilinged parlour this morning, and let it burn all day to take the chill off.

Tacker was simply thankful for Miss Lumley's good sense. He didn't like the parlour at the best of times. He had come home from school after all, drawn by warmth and the thought of an extra meal, with cakes and jam, and accepted the ordeal of being smartened up because he did want to see Miss Lumley.

He was glad to note that going away had not smartened *her* up at all. She was dressed in a drab-coloured, drooping tweed coat and skirt with a thickly knitted woollen jumper underneath, her old, familiar stout brown lace-up shoes, and thick, fawn-coloured lisle stockings. She wore no adornment of any kind, and one of her earphone buns looked as though it might come adrift at any moment.

But so far she had only spoken a few words to him, and her manner had been stiff and formal. It did not occur to him that she was capable of any kind of shyness, and so he resigned himself to the thought that she preferred to talk to his mother.

He ate his tea and listened. They talked about the puppy. He had expected Miss Lumley to bring it with her, and was disappointed to learn that she had left it at the Rifle House.

'It's a relief to have it settled,' Miss Lumley said. 'At least I've ensured that it has a good home.'

'Ah, well, the lady that give it to you would be glad to think it was with people that know about dogs, and that the little girl has taken a fancy to it.'

Little girl, thought Tacker, regarding his mother wonderingly. Did she mean Sarah? She was no more a little girl than he was a little boy. Well, if Miss Lumley had given the puppy to Sarah, he wasn't likely to see it.

'So tiny it is,' Mrs Venn was saying. 'I never did see such a little thing. No bigger than that.' She turned to Tacker and showed him the palm of her hand. 'It can sit on my hand. And soft – softer than velvet, even.'

'But you said it was a greyhound,' Tacker objected. 'Greyhounds aren't small.'

'*Italian* Greyhound. That's a special sort. They only weigh eight or nine pounds, full grown, Mrs Wickham said.'

Tacker tried to imagine this very small greyhound, but found it difficult.

'What use are they?' he asked.

'No *practical* use at all,' said Miss Lumley. 'Just pets.'

Mrs Venn asked a question about Cornwall, and Tacker's attention drifted away from their talk. He looked out at the early dark. A boy on a bicycle shot past, followed by another; he could just make out that they were Georgie Hancock and Bill Heard, the boy who acquired a bicycle last month. He felt a new pang of envy. If only Miss Lumley still lived here, and he could work for her again, and somehow persuade his mother to let him keep the money he earned this time – for a month or two, at least!

His mother offered him a piece of cake, and as he took it he became aware of what they were saying.

'If my brother marries again, I shall be back, you may be sure,' Miss Lumley said. 'And it looks as though he will.'

Come back? It was magic. He'd just been hoping she would come back and now. . . . Tacker listened closely.

'I shouldn't have been in such a hurry to sell the Rifle House,' Miss Lumley went on.

'Well, there, you did it for the best. You weren't to know,' Mrs Venn observed.

'Anyway, don't be surprised if I write to ask you to look out for a cottage for me, in a month or two. Something to rent this time, I think. Then I can take my time in house-hunting.'

'I'll look around for you, and welcome. Come the summer, there's usually a cottage or two to offer.'

Miss Lumley inclined her head, and turned to Tacker, who had been staring at her as he listened to this exchange. She seemed suddenly to realize that she had hardly spoken to him.

'Sarah tells me you have a pet owl. May I see it?'

Tacker went red. This was what came of boasting. 'He's gone off wild, like, now it's winter,' he said desperately, thankful that his mother, refilling teacups, did not appear to have heard.

Noting that this was a subject which, for some reason she could not guess, caused embarrassment, Miss Lumley did not pursue it, and turned to Mrs Venn again.

When tea was over, she seemed in no hurry to leave, and Mrs Venn tried not to be seen glancing at the clock as the hands crept towards six, and she thought of the meal she should be preparing for her husband.

It was five to six when Miss Lumley finally said good-bye. Alec Venn came in as Tacker was carrying the stacked tray of tea things through the back door.

'She gone?' he asked in a low voice, jerking his head towards the sitting-room. Tacker nodded.

'That's good.' He opened the kitchen door for his son and shut it behind them.

'There, I'm all behind,' said Mrs Venn.

'Not so much as all that,' her husband said, giving her a pat of unusual playfulness.

'Oh, get along with you. You know what I mean. I'm late.'

While he washed with water dipped from the black pot heated on the range, she began to tell him about the tea party, and Tacker wondered why she did it; she must know as well as he did that his father wasn't interested in such things.

'That brother of hers may marry again, looks like. Hasn't wasted much time, has he? And if he does, Miss Lumley'll be back here in no time, she says.'

'Oh ah,' her husband responded, not really heeding, as usual. But Tacker, finishing off a slice of left-over bread and butter, thought that with any luck she would be living in Hamblecombe again by next summer. Never had a wish been more swiftly granted. The trouble was, if she happened to rent a cottage with water laid on, and only a small garden, there'd be no way for him to earn bicycle money from her. But never mind, as long as she came, there was hope of *something* – and in any case, he found he was glad to know she might be coming.

Eleven

Early on Christmas Morning

Two days before Christmas Mrs Venn sat by the fire and wrapped up family presents. Tacker worked at a model Tiger Moth on a sheet of newspaper spread out on the brown chenille tablecloth. He had just come in from the street, where he and some of the others had been watching Georgie Hancock trying unsuccessfully to get his acetylene cycle lamp to work. The smell of wet carbide and frost was still in his nostrils. He had come home past the Queen's Arms where, through one of the heart-shaped holes in the bar's wooden shutters, he had seen his father playing in the semi-finals of a table skittles match; the final would be tomorrow, Christmas Eve.

'There, there's Granfer's,' Mrs Venn said with satisfaction, adding a small parcel of tobacco and hand-knitted socks to the pile beside her. 'I want for you to go over and give him that, Tacker, early Christmas morning.'

'Me?' Tacker looked round in alarm. 'You coming too?'

'No need for me to come, is there?'

'You always have.'

'Well, yes, but I reckon you're old enough now to take your grandfather his presents without me being there.'

'I won't know what to say.'

'What to say? Bless me, boy, say "Merry Christmas".

You don't need for to make a speech. You're not scared of Granfer all of a sudden, are you?'

'Well, no, but – '

'But what? You don't go over to see him like you used, is that it?'

'He doesn't like me no more.'

'Doesn't like you? What a thing to say. He likes you well enough, and you've hurt his feelings, that's what it is.'

Guilt, heavy as raw dough, dropped into Tacker's stomach.

'I aren't done nothing,' he muttered like a four-year-old.

'You know what you've done and not done. You go over on Christmas morning and see what happens.'

And so, two mornings later, in the cockcrow dark, with only a slice of bread and butter and a cup of tea inside him, Tacker set off for his grandfather's cottage. He had not been given his own presents yet; he had been told that present-giving was to be at breakfast time this year. He couldn't for the life of him imagine why he was being sent out so early; usually they all went to Granfer's about midday. The reason his mother had given him was that his grandfather always got up early, and at his age he was not likely to receive anything much by post, so it would be nice for him to have his presents early.

It was a morning of black frost under a cloudy sky, and daylight came slowly. From most cottage windows he passed, lamplight or candle-light shone out, some upstairs, some down. He was surprised when he reached his grandfather's cottage to see that *his* light was still upstairs, since, as his mother had reminded him, his grandfather was usually up early. Was he ill?

The outer door was not locked. It never was. Few

villagers locked their doors; they did not steal from one another, and did not possess anything they thought an outsider might want to steal. Inside, corridor and stair-well were dark.

Tacker called 'Granfer?'

'Tacker? Come up then. I'm still in bed.'

The boy groped his way up the short, steep flight of stairs, opened the door of his grandfather's room and advanced uncertainly to the bedside. 'Merry Christmas this is for you,' he said in one breath, and put the package on the counterpane.

'Merry Christmas,' the old man said. He was smoking his first pipe of the day. He took it out of his mouth and propped it in the tray of the flowery china candlestick beside him while he picked up the package and turned it over in his hands.

'What's this, eh? Present? Your Mam send you? That's it, then. Now, seeing I'm a bit slow this morning, will you do something for me?' He handed Tacker a box of matches. 'Go down and put a light to the oil stove, and set the kettle on for me tea, will you?'

Tacker hesitated. 'You all right?'

'All right? I'm proper. Christmas lie-in, that's all.'

Tacker went carefully down the stairs and along to the tiny kitchen. Outside the closed door he stopped in surprise. Under the latch was a small hole, and yellow light showed through. Who had lighted the kitchen lamp, if his grandfather had not been down? It could not have burned all night – it would have run out of oil. He listened. No sound. Was someone there? He was fearful and yet curious, and he longed to run upstairs again. But that would look daft.

Cautiously he raised the latch and peered into the room. The lamp burned on the table; there was no one there, but propped against the table stood a bicycle. Completely bewildered, he gazed at it. A *bicycle*, in Granfer's kitchen? He didn't ride a bicycle. Or at least he hadn't for a long time – not since the night he tumbled off into the stream in Combascott, before the wall was built alongside the village street. Tacker could remember hearing about that; he had been about four at the time. But what had happened to Granfer's bike after that he did not know.

This one was not new, but it gleamed with a fresh coat of yellow enamel, picked out with white. The handlebars and wheel rims shone bright; the tyres looked unused. There was no pump or lamp. Pinned to the saddle was a piece of paper.

He went forward and read the message on it.

'For Tacker.
Happy Christmas
from Granfer.'

A bicycle. *Now.* He did not need to wait until his birthday, after all. And it was his grandfather who had given it to him! This, he supposed, was what his mother meant when she sometimes spoke of 'coals of fire'. All the same, it seemed plain that it was his mother who had fixed it. She had told the old man he wanted a bicycle; got round him to do it up.

He crouched down, examining it. It had been beautifully cared for, oiled and greased and kept free from rust, even before it was repainted. But his grandfather always took care of things; he liked to tell of the way he had cared for his fine stallions when he walked them as a younger man. The churchyard, tended by him, was well weeded and full of flowers, and he scythed the grass close, even on such forgotten graves as John Hobson's.

Tacker stood up and took hold of the hand-grips, and

bounced the front wheel on its deep-patterned tyres. His, his, his. He could ride out, down the street, all round the village like the others did (and as he had done before now, but only on borrowed bikes); round and round, swooping and whooping. He turned, ready to wheel it out, but remembered. He hadn't even said thank you.

The door opened and his grandfather came in. He had put on trousers and the fisherman's jersey he wore for gardening on his allotment.

'Well, will it do?' he asked.

Tacker did a thing he had not done for a long time. He flung his arms round his grandfather and hugged him. He said 'Thank 'ee, Granfer, thank 'ee,' over and over again.

'Ah, so I'm not such a bad old feller after all?'

'I'm sorry.' Inarticulate as ever, Tacker could offer no more than this for all the months of neglect, but the old man was satisfied.

'Well then, no more to be said. But you can ride round on that machine and see me now and again in future. There, look, you aren't lit me stove.'

He struck a match, opened the oil stove's little mica window and touched the flame to the wick. He chuckled.

'We had you on properly, didn't us?'

Tacker wrenched his attention from the bicycle and began to realize. The cryptic asides between his father and grandfather on the morning of the ghosty frost; his mother's unexpected request that he should take his grandfather's present to him; his grandfather's request for him to light the stove, in a kitchen where the oil lamp had already been lit. He grinned, and the old man, delighted, said, 'We had 'ee there, didn't us? We had 'ee there.'

He ran a finger over the newly enamelled mudguards. 'I'm sorry I couldn't manage to put on a pump, and a lamp.'

'That don't matter,' Tacker said, thinking that the lamp, at least, mattered a good deal; as he couldn't ride after dark without it, that meant that at this time of year he wouldn't be able to go out after four o'clock.

'You've done it up handsome,' he said. 'Is it the bike that – is it the one you used to ride?'

The old man nodded. 'That's the one. They say I'd had a few in the Crown that night, don't um? Well, I hadn't. One pint, I'd had. It was a wet night, and dark and slippy, and I came off in the stream. Didn't hurt the bike much, but it shook me bones. Wet to the skin, I was, and cold, so I got rheumatiz. Just didn't ever want to ride the thing again, after that. But I kept it put away. Might have changed me mind – never know.'

'Where did you keep it?' Tacker had been puzzling over this; why hadn't he seen it on any of his visits to the cottage?

The old man jerked his head towards the ceiling. 'Up over.'

Tacker had not even seen inside his grandfather's bedroom for a long time, until this morning; the second of the two upstairs rooms had always been a mystery. He had heard his mother say it was full of junk, and she would dearly like to give it a turn out, if she was let. If he had known there was a bicycle there, he thought. . . . And yet in a way he was glad he hadn't known; it would have spoilt this present.

'Time you were off home,' his grandfather said. 'Your Mam'll have breakfast ready, and be after me for keeping you. I'll step over later, tell her.'

He saw Tacker to the gate. 'You can ride that thing, I suppose?'

Tacker swung a leg over the saddle to show him.

'Um. Beats me how you all learn it. Well, straight home, mind. Don't go gallivanting off.'

Tacker only smiled by way of answer, and waved as he let the cycle carry him away downhill until he was out of sight. Go straight home on his first ride on his own bicycle? Of course not. He must have one circuit of the village, at least.

He hoped to meet Archie or Georgie or one of the others. Disappointingly, the street was empty. By this time, every villager was either at church, opening parcels, or eating breakfast.

He stood up out of the saddle and rushed full tilt down the hill below the forge; then pedalled hard up the opposite slope, and just reached the top without dismounting. Sharp right along the north ridge, past cob walls, stone walls, hedges, and then round the corner by the dipping place and so home.

Elated, hungry, and breathless, he ran into the indoor warmth.

His mother came out of the kitchen and smiled broadly at sight of him.

'You managed that errand for me, did you?' she asked.

He hugged her, too. 'It's lovely, the bike. I never guessed. Have you seen it, all done up? Come and look. Where's Ernie? I want to show him.'

'Ah that'll do later. Breakfast's keeping warm on the range. Come in and we'll have our presents before anything else.'

Ernie, at home for two days' holiday, was given his first. (Molly was not home yet; she would be coming tomorrow. Her employer had decided she could not spare her until the arduous business of Christmas dinner was safely out of the way.)

Then it was Tacker's turn to be given his parcels. He opened the two from his parents first. In one was a bicycle pump; in the other, a lamp.

Twelve

A Small Find

Sarah lay in bed and watched the rain. She felt she had been doing this for months, although it was only early February and the wet weather had not set in until the New Year. The voice of the stream was louder than she had ever heard it, and she wondered how deep it was now. She had not seen it since the Christmas holidays.

One evening soon after the beginning of term she had felt sick and heavy, and woken next morning to see small blisters the shape of rice grains on her arms. The school doctor said 'Chickenpox', and Sarah was hurried away to the sanatorium, where in a day or two she was joined by others. Half the school had it, she heard, but by this time she was home, convalescing – and for the first time in her life, in no hurry to be well after an illness. She did not want to go back to school.

The reason for this lay under the coverlet on her bed: Miss Lumley's unwanted present, the Italian Greyhound puppy. Sarah had named her Biri, for no reason except that the name occurred to her and sounded vaguely Italian.

The puppy, three months old by this time, was still very small. She was of the colour known to breeders as peach-fawn, and had little clown's eyebrows, like accents circumflex. There was hardly any trace in her yet of the delicate lines of the adult dog. Her ears were still roughly triangular stubs against her head; her stomach was round and full, and her skin loose on her, as though made a few sizes too large to allow for growth.

Sarah would sometimes pleat a fold of it across the back of her neck, while the puppy nuzzled her hand and rolled smoke-grey eyes at her. She found it hard to understand that Miss Lumley had had no wish to keep this beautiful little creature.

For Sarah, Biri absorbed the loneliness of the past few months. But her love for the puppy was mixed with fear: she was afraid that, while she was away at school, Biri would get out into the road and be run over, or wander into the fields, like Budge, and be caught in a trap. The memory of the sea-mist morning came back to her again and again, as she played with Biri or looked at her, curled asleep.

Budge's savage wound had healed, but one of the saw-toothed gins could kill a puppy as small and fine-boned as Biri.

The trouble was that callers repeatedly left the solid wooden gate open, so that any dog that happened to be in the garden was tempted to slip into the road. The kennel dogs were secure in their exercise runs. But twice during the winter, a dog brought up to the house for one reason or another had run into the road. Each time it had been noticed at once, and brought back – but Biri was so small, so easy to miss . . .

Later that morning the clouds lightened and began to show breaks of steamy blue. The February sunshine, like watered honey, slanted across the dripping landscape. A fire burned in the room that had been Miss Lumley's sitting-room. Sarah, up and dressed, sat there, on the window seat, and stared out.

Once or twice lately, sitting here with Biri asleep on her

lap, she had seen Tacker go flying past on his bicycle, alone or followed by two or three other boys. She had heard about the bicycle from Mrs Venn, who had not been able to resist talking about it on her first visit to the Rifle House after Christmas. So Tacker was one of the cycling bravoes who rode hands-off around the village, shouting to one another in what might as well have been another language; she could never make out a word of it.

She would have been surprised if anyone had told her that her possession of a bicycle, when he hadn't one, had been one of the things that had made Tacker unwilling to be friendly.

Biri sat down near the door and began to whimper and shiver a little, a sign that she needed to go out; she had been

quickly house-trained. Sarah opened the door into the hall. She saw her Wellingtons lying in a corner, and on an impulse put them on and took her old 'home' coat from its hook.

With the puppy following, she went slowly down the stepped path towards the stream. The garden narrowed to a little grass plot where the bank was at its lowest. She leaned against the trunk of an elm that grew there, and looked into the gulley.

The clear, shallow stream she had known was gone. Water flowed, fast and deep, murky with silt and scuds of yeasty froth, and at intervals fretted against miniature log-jams of sticks, straw, rusty fern, and dead leaves.

Biri sniffed near the edge, walking delicately as a fawn in wet grass. Sarah picked her up, full of a new fear that she would tumble into this swift brown current and be drowned – because there was no longer any path to save her if she fell over the bank. Nothing was left of all the work of last summer and autumn. In a few weeks, the stream had washed away the path and triumphantly reclaimed its old course.

By the end of February, Sarah was told she was well enough to go back to school. She thought of taking Biri and running away, but she was not a child for the extravagant gesture, the vehement protest. She could only say urgently to her mother, 'Take care of Biri. Don't let anyone leave the gate open.'

At school she lived for Friday afternoons, and the putt-putt of the Trojan coming up the tree-lined road to fetch her home.

March brought warm days, and with sunshine and better health she worried less. Term was almost over, and then, for four weeks, she would be able to look after Biri herself.

So the shock was all the worse when her father, driving her home on the last Friday of term, told her that some prospective buyers had called that afternoon to look at a litter of Corgi puppies; unnoticed, they had left the gate ajar, and Biri had slipped out and not yet returned.

All through that January and February, on any reasonably fine day, the cycling boys had been out. There were five of them by this time; Tacker had been chagrined to find that two others, beside himself, had acquired bicycles at Christmas. Out of school hours they circled the village repeatedly, clockwise or anti-clockwise, as the mood took them, or raced from the shop to the forge and back again.

Sometimes, at week-ends, they were off seawards to Combascott. Tacker would glance swiftly at the windows of the Rifle House in passing; he never saw Sarah looking out, and wondered if she had nevertheless seen his bicycle. From his mother, he heard of her illness.

'Very low-spirited, her is, after that chicken-pox,' Mrs Venn reported. 'Proper mopey and out of sorts. Only thing that cheers her up is having that there little dog.'

Tacker had never seen the little dog, but his mother, who was amazed and amused by it, gave him details of each stage of its development.

When it rained, Tacker did not take his bike out. He spent much of his time in the barn, where he kept the machine, polishing the enamel work, the handlebars and wheel rims, and oiling it until it oozed from the hubs. He seldom saw the owl these days, and supposed it had found some other, lonelier barn, perhaps out in the fields, that it liked better.

Once or twice a week he would wander through the churchyard, if his grandfather was working there, and chat to him. On rainy evenings he visited him at his cottage, and the old man persuaded him to play draughts or dominoes, or taught him cribbage.

Apart from visits to Combascott, or rides down the old limeburner's lane to the beach there, the cycling gang did not go far afield, and it was not until the lighter, warmer days of March that it occurred to Tacker that, as he could ride as far in ten minutes as he had once been able to walk in an hour, he had a new freedom. He could visit places that had formerly been a rare bus-ride away – Barlingford, or Hillacombe, the port at which the paddle-steamers called in summer. He could even ride up into the high downland country that stretched away eastwards for thirty miles until it merged with the moors.

He had no map, and wouldn't have been able to read one if he had, so he never knew where he was going when he set off on one of his solitary rides. Sometimes, as it began to grow dark, he became a little afraid. The high-hedged lanes seemed to twist away endlessly into unknown country, and even the signposts, when he came to them, pointed to hamlets he had never heard of. He was reduced to asking his way, and was scolded for coming home late to high tea.

Asked where he had been, he would only say, 'Riding round.' Riding round *where*, his mother wanted to know – but he hardly knew himself. She would sigh, and talk of getting his father to speak to him, or perhaps taking the bicycle away from him for a week or two until he learned more sense.

One Friday at the end of March, the sun burned through the school room windows all the afternoon as though it were May, and Tacker felt more than usually a prisoner there. The moment school was over he rushed out, seized his bicycle and swung himself into its saddle. Spinning along between hedges stippled with opening leaf buds, he shouted aloud, or sang in his hoarse tuneless voice a tuneless song.

He did not mean to go too far afield, though. The last time he had been on one of these jaunts he had reached home so late that his mother, vexed with worry, had said that she would lock his bike away if he did it again – and she had sounded as though she meant it.

At sunset he was free-wheeling along the side of a narrow valley that ran down obliquely to join the Combascott road. He was used to seeing small animals on these almost traffic-less, unmacadamed ways: stoats, shrews, young rabbits. But now, far ahead in the pinkish evening light, he saw a creature that puzzled him. It wasn't the shape of anything he knew. He began to pedal, not really expecting to reach whatever it was before it ran or hopped into the hedge and was gone to some hiding place. But it trotted along, and stopped now and then to lift a paw and sniff the air in an uncertain way. It was dog-like – yet what dog could be so small, so fine-legged? What dog except the tiny greyhound puppy, with the foreign name, that Miss Lumley had given Sarah?

He had not heard of its loss, earlier that afternoon. He expected to see Sarah somewhere on the road ahead. But there was no one. He realized that the puppy must have strayed away from the kennels – like Budge, he thought, remembering that morning last summer.

With his own recent experiences of losing his way, he felt sorry for the puppy. How small it was! It glanced round fearfully as he drew near, and began to run. Cycling, he had the advantage in speed, but it struck him that it might be just as well if he could drive it at least as far as the main road. If he caught it there, he would have more than a mile of riding or pushing his bicycle one-handed and carrying the puppy with the other. He imagined it would struggle.

As he followed it slowly, he thought he would like to keep it as his own pet. What if he didn't take it back to the Rifle House? Hid it somewhere?

But he saw at once it was impossible. Where *could* he hide it? In the barn? It would cry and his mother would find it. She had not often been seriously angry with him, but if he tried such a thing, she would be. No, the puppy would have to go back where it – or she, he corrected himself, looking at her more closely – belonged.

When he saw the main road ahead he pedalled fast, jumped off, pushed his bicycle into the hedge and ran back to scoop up Biri before she realized what was happening.

He tried and failed to button her into his jacket; it was not loose enough. But he held her against him, inside it, fastened the bottom button and pushed his bicycle with one hand while he supported the bulge that was Biri with the other.

It was uphill to the Rifle House, but not far. He left his bicycle outside the gate and knocked at the door. It seemed odd not to walk in, after giving a brief rap, as he had in Miss Lumley's day.

He waited, and no one came. Biri trembled against his ribs. He knocked again, louder, and still no one came. Of course, they would be out looking for the puppy – but there might be someone at the kennels. He went round the corner of the house and looked down the garden. A movement in one of the fields high above the farm caught his eye. It was Sarah, walking slowly along a hedgeside, her shoulders sagging in dejection.

He whistled and waved. She stopped, trying to focus the sound. When she seemed to be looking straight at him, Tacker held up Biri.

Sarah began to run. In a minute she was out of sight behind the elms. He went down the garden to meet her. At

the top of the steps leading to the old dipping place he paused and looked down at the swift water. No sign of a path; had Sarah given up building it, or had it been washed away?

Sarah splashed into the stream in the meadow. He saw she was still wearing school clothes, and Wellingtons. As she ducked under the pole-and-thorn barrier she shipped water into her boots and tore the back of her gym tunic. She took no notice of these things, and quickly waded the last few yards.

'Biri!' she exclaimed. Tacker gave her the puppy and she hugged and fondled it. 'Oh, Biri! Oh, Biri! Oh, Tacker, thank you!'

The puppy licked her ear, her neck, her cheek. 'How did you find her? Where was she?'

'Up Old Cleave.'

'Did you know she was lost? Were you looking for her?'

'No. I was just riding round.'

'You've got a nice bike. I saw you go past last Saturday.'

Sarah rubbed her chin against Biri's silken head. 'I wish I didn't have to go away to school. No one looks after Biri properly, except me. I knew this would happen. I *hate* school.'

She didn't altogether, but at this moment felt she did.

Tacker, who took it for granted that everyone hated school, made no comment. He was looking along the gulley. Here and there little ledges of hard-packed earth stuck out from the bank. There *had* been a path all the way, and the flooding winter stream had carried it down to the sea.

Sarah followed his gaze. 'I finished the path,' she said. 'I built it the whole way, from the waterfall down to here. But after all that rain. . . .' She waved a hand; he could see for himself.

'Want to build it up again? I'll help you,' Tacker said.

'*Would* you, Tacker? Yes, but you said once before you'd come and help, but you didn't.'

'I never.' Tacker could not remember committing himself at any time.

'You did. The day we found Budge. That afternoon, in the churchyard, I asked if you'd come and help, and you said all right.'

'Well, I will this time.'

Sarah was still sceptical. 'You've got a bike now. You'll always want to go riding off somewhere.'

'You've got a bike too, and you did the path,' he pointed out.

She was just about to answer that she had had hers for some time, and got used to it, but saw it wouldn't be tactful, and stopped in time.

'I'll come,' he assured her. *Now* he could do it. He was a bicycle owner, and a proved fighter, and he could build a path down the Great Green Gorge of the Orinoco, a high, strong path that would defy the winter floods. He would have started that minute, only he saw that they would need to wait until the water level fell a little. Also it was getting late; the light was failing, and there was still that threat of having his bike locked up.

'I'll come Saturdays, when you're back from school,' he said.

'It'll be the holidays after next Wednesday.'

'I'll come Saturdays anyway.'

They both heard a sound; the putt-putt of the Trojan coming up the road.

'They've been out searching for Biri,' Sarah said.

They went up the garden together. At the top, Tacker grinned at her.

'Us'll make that path proper this time,' he said.

Thirteen

From the Source to the Sea

It did not occur to either Sarah or Tacker that he should present himself at the front door of the Rifle House and ask for her, when he came to help with the stream path. They both took it for granted that he would arrive in his usual way, along the course of the stream. If Sarah was not there, he would begin work without her. She kept a rake, a mattock and a square-bladed spade, all borrowed from her father's tool store, under the elm tree nearest the waterfall.

He was construction engineer, navvy, and foreman by turns. He was not content, as Sarah had been, to rake up an inch or two of small stones from the stream bed to form a foundation; he insisted that they should collect every big stone they could find – there were a good many at the foot of the fall, and others scattered farther down – and use them as a kind of outer work. Smaller stones were shovelled behind. Only when the foundations were well clear of the water would he consent to put on a top surface of earth and weeds. Grass tussocks dug up from the upper garden turfed it well.

During the village school's short Easter holiday, Tacker came two or three times a week. When he was not there, Sarah worked on, trying to keep to his stern specifications, and feeling a little nervous of his critical eye, the next time he came. She always had Biri with her. She put an old piece of matting on the finished section of the path, and Biri sat on this and watched her, or curled up and slept.

After a dry March, the water level was falling rapidly. Primroses were out along the bank, bluebells and pussy willows were in bud, and fern fronds uncurling. It wasn't the garden she had planned, Sarah thought, but it was pretty as it was. Planting could come later.

She and Tacker did not talk very much as they worked together, except for a few words about the work itself, and it was some time before Mr and Mrs Wickham heard voices and discovered that Tacker had become a frequent visitor to the garden.

'I never see him arrive,' Mrs Wickham said. 'Do you let him in, Sarah?'

Sarah explained.

'He should come to the door and ask for you properly,' her mother said.

Sarah felt certain that if Tacker was made to come formally, he would not come at all. She begged her mother not to insist on it. 'And don't say anything to Mrs Venn, either. *Please*,' she said.

'But I really don't see that he need be so secretive.'

Sarah tried to think of a reason for what seemed to her a perfectly natural way of behaving. 'He's shy,' she said. And realized that, in an odd way, this was true.

Her mother gave way reluctantly, doubtfully, and the path-building went on steadily.

One Saturday morning in June, Sarah told Tacker she had heard from Miss Lumley. He felt a spurt of jealousy. It was a long time since Miss Lumley had written to him – but then he did not write to her. Sarah had told him that she wrote now and then to tell Miss Lumley how Biri was getting on.

'She's coming back to live here,' Sarah went on.

'I know. Her told us, that time back in the winter.'

'Yes, but it's definite now. Her brother *has* got married again. I expect Miss Lumley was quite glad.'

Tacker grunted. He did not want to talk to Sarah about Miss Lumley, and he felt resentful that she had known Miss Lumley's plans before he did.

The next day Mrs Venn received a letter from Miss Lumley, asking her if she knew of a cottage to let in either of the valley villages.

'Well, now, let's see. Can you call one to mind, Alec?' she asked her husband.

'What about Mrs Tucker's? That's stood empty since last September.'

'Mill Cottage, do you mean, down to Combascott? That 'ud do. It's got a bathroom and all.'

So that evening Mrs Venn wrote to Miss Lumley in her carefully formed handwriting, and some time later Miss Lumley wrote back to thank her and tell her that she had arranged to rent Mill Cottage.

She would not want his help there, Tacker thought, when he heard; Mill Cottage had water laid on, and a very small garden. But what did that matter? He did not need to earn bicycle money now.

By the time she came back, she would have been away a year. He remembered his truanting day, after she had left the Rifle House – and was amazed to think how long it was since he had played truant. The last time must have been – when? In the autumn, when school seemed unbearable after the open-air life of harvest.

A fine warm spell around mid-summer tempted him to go off for a day on his bicycle. But he realized with dismay that he was caught; the bicycle itself had become his warrant for good behaviour. It would be forfeit for a day's truanting, that was certain. Morning after morning he longed to cycle away into the country – but he always turned towards school in the end.

During the long light evenings the cycling gang, Tacker among them, swooped and circled like the swallows flying high over their heads. One thundery Sunday at the beginning of July they made one of their impulsive descents on Combascott.

As they rushed along a straight stretch of road outside the village, Tacker suddenly saw Miss Lumley walking towards them. So she was back. She must have moved into Mill Cottage. She looked at him and he made as though to put on his brakes – but did not. Stiff-faced, he shot past. He told himself he couldn't stop – couldn't leave the others.

The instant he was past, guilt gripped him. He glanced back furtively. Miss Lumley had stopped and was looking back too. His cheeks burned.

At that moment Archie shouted something that made the others guffaw. It wasn't about Miss Lumley – Tacker did not think any of them had even noticed her – but *she* might think they were jeering at her, and that he, Tacker, was joining in.

In bed that night he went over the incident a dozen times. He knew very clearly by this time why he hadn't stopped: because he hadn't been able to face being seen, by the others, talking to Miss Lumley. It was the old dread of being teased.

But suddenly he knew something else. He didn't mind so much about teasing any more. Most of the boys of his own age were by this time a little wary of him. In the months when several of them had been longing to own bicycles, they had begun to call him Bantam, because he had been readiest of all to push a quarrel to a fight. The reputation he had gained then had been an armour ever since.

But out of old stupid habit he had passed Miss Lumley, 'like as if he was too proud to know her,' he told himself. What could he do about it? He wanted to talk to someone. Not his mother; he knew too well what she would say: 'Go down to Mill Cottage this minute and apologize.' Sarah? But he wouldn't see Sarah until next Saturday; she would be going to school in the morning. His grandfather? No, not if it was something about one of his 'Rifle House friends'. His father?

He thought about his father, who found it so difficult to scold him, and was abashed by a show of affection, and did not like having to entertain visitors. Perhaps this was a thing his father would understand better than anyone.

That evening, when Alec Venn was working in the garden, Tacker went out to help. He took time to get up courage to say anything.

Finally he began: 'Da? You know Miss Lumley?'

'Her's back again, I heard. Funny old girl. Like her, don't you?'

'Her's all right.' Perhaps he had been wrong; perhaps his father wasn't the right one to talk to. All the same, Tacker plunged on, 'We was going down to Combascott last night on our bikes. Miss Lumley was coming up the road. She saw me. I didn't stop. Didn't look at her proper, even.'

He waited for some reaction, but his father said nothing.

'I don't want to go and say I'm sorry,' Tacker added quickly. 'It 'ud look worse, I reckon. Like as if I'd done it a-purpose and only been sorry afterwards.'

Alec Venn sighed quietly and Tacker, glancing at him, was suddenly comforted by the idea that his father was remembering a time when he had done the same sort of thing to someone.

'What are you going to do about it, then?'

No reproaches; no advice, either. Just a question. What *was* he going to do about it? That was what he had hoped to be told.

'If I was to go down and see her – and tell her we was having a race – and I'd passed her before I'd seen it was her . . .'

'Mm. Something of that. As long as you go and speak. Show you didn't mean it.'

This, it seemed, was all the guidance he was going to get. But it was enough to reassure him, and so, the next afternoon after school, he set off, alone, for Combascott. He cycled unusually slowly, still not sure just what he was going to say, or that he would have the courage to say it at all.

It had been a day of thunder-showers, and between the thick green hedges the road steamed under a slaty sky. Mutterings among the clouds seemed to be echoed in Tacker's stomach. At every bend in the road he was tempted to turn back. But he reached Mill Cottage and dismounted. He went up the short path to the door and gave a tentative tap.

No one came, and he rapped louder. Over the wall dividing the Mill Cottage garden from its neighbour he could see a middle-aged couple moving about. They were strangers – holiday visitors, he thought. The man was watering the flower beds, the woman picking roses.

The man looked up and saw Tacker. He came to the wall and leaned on it.

'Got a message for Miss Lumley, sonny?' he asked. 'She's out. Gone out painting.'

Tacker disliked very much being called sonny. He merely

shook his head in answer. He was surprised to hear the man refer to Miss Lumley by name, but he supposed she had got to know these people as fellow-gardeners, over the wall.

'You wanted to tell Miss Lumley something, did you?' the man insisted encouragingly, as though Tacker might be a little slow-witted.

Tacker's impulse was to mumble, 'It don't matter,' and go away. But suddenly he told himself that mumbling and going away was for little 'uns. He was too old for that.

'Yes,' he said. 'But I'll tell her later. I'll come back.'

'And who shall I say called?' the man asked, in a special voice like a butler in a play, and Tacker knew he was being made fun of, and began to dislike the holidaymaker very much.

'Tack – ' he began, and stopped himself. Not to this chap, who seemed to think village boys were daft. 'Tom,' he said. He didn't like Thomas, because he thought it sounded stuffy, and he liked Tommy even less. 'Tom Venn.' He drew himself up and the gift of tongues descended upon him. In a clear voice, rather too loud he said, 'Please tell Miss Lumley that Tom Venn wanted to talk to her.'

He couldn't believe it. Had he really spoken up like that?

Straight-backed, he turned about and marched to the gate. He'd done his best. The holiday chap would at least give Miss Lumley the message, he supposed, and she might guess why he had come. He'd see her some other time – tomorrow, perhaps. No, not tomorrow; that was Saturday, and he was doing something special. Well then, some time.

The next morning Tacker sat in the sun on the warm turf of the Sailor's Grave, waiting for Sarah, who was having her Saturday music lesson at the Rectory. When it was over, they meant to set out for Combascott by way of the stream, to follow its course, as Sarah had once suggested they should, all the way to the sea. They were taking food to eat on the beach. They had planned this the previous Sunday; the path was not finished, but it was going well, and they felt it could be left to itself for one Saturday.

The thought that he and Sarah would almost certainly be seen together, and there might be teasing later, no longer bothered him. He felt confident he could deal with that.

Along the wall beside him, fuchsia was in flower. He stretched out an arm and popped a few of the fat red buds; then leaned back and looked up at the gleaming hands of the church clock. Still ten minutes to wait. He need not have come out so early, but at home his mother was bustling around, tidying up before she left for her morning's work at the Rifle House, and it was best to be out of the way.

He heard footsteps in the street, and peered through the fuchsia. Miss Lumley was coming down the hill, carrying a bulging brown paper bag. To his surprise she stopped at the door of Bray Cottage and knocked. Was she going to ask his mother to come to work for her again?

The door opened, and there stood his mother in her apron.

'Oh, Miss Lumley, it's nice to see you back. How have you been keeping? Step in a minute, will you?'

'No, thank you, I won't stop. I know you're busy. I was passing this way, so I thought I might leave this for Tacker. I saw it in Cornwall and thought he might like it.'

Tacker had no difficulty in hearing what was said, but he couldn't see what it was Miss Lumley had brought him. He leaned forward, eager to catch a glimpse of it.

His mother took the brown paper bag with expressions of thanks, and looked inside.

'Oh, M'm, you shouldn't! Isn't that pretty? I'll give it to

him so soon as he comes in, but he went out not long since, and he's off down to Combascott. Took a picnic and all, so he won't be back till late. But he'll be ever so pleased, I know. Fairly wonderful, how they do it, isn't it?'

What was it, Tacker wondered. He longed to declare himself; run across the road and see the present. Yet an odd reluctance held him back; as always he preferred to talk to Miss Lumley alone, not in his mother's presence.

She had brought him a present – so she couldn't be annoyed with him. Even though she had bought it in Cornwall, before she came to Mill Cottage, she hadn't changed her mind about giving it to him.

His mother lifted the thing in her hands and examined it closely; the glint of glass caught his eye, and he saw what it was: a ship in a bottle.

There was one in the window of a cottage in Combascott; it was the only one he had ever seen until this moment. He would put his on the window-sill of his bedroom, below the bottle-glass pane, and every morning when he woke, it would be there to look at.

If he didn't go across now, he would have to wait until he came back from the beach to see and handle it, see hull and sails and rigging miraculously complete inside the glass. Still he did not move.

His mother was asking, 'Are you settling in at Mill Cottage, Miss Lumley? I hope you find it suits, seeing as I recommended it?'

'It suits me to a T, Mrs Venn, thank you. It's a more sensible size than the Rifle House, just for one. I may stay there indefinitely. Well, I must be going in search of a good view for my next calendar. I expect I shall see Tacker about in the village one of these days. He has a bicycle now, hasn't he?'

'That bicycle! Him and the others, they race around like mad things. I never know whether he'll come home safe or no.'

'I don't expect he'll come to much harm. He seems well able to look after himself.'

Miss Lumley said good-bye and turned to go up the street again. Tacker watched her pass, stalwart and lonely, as she had always been. He scrambled to his feet. He would run after her, talk to her, explain things before, in some mysterious way, it was too late.

But at that moment he heard footsteps on the gravel of the churchyard path, and turned to see Sarah, with Biri on a lead beside her, coming round the west end of the church.

Miss Lumley went out of sight at the top of the hill. There was no time for explanations, after all.

Sarah saw him and waved. He waved back and ran down between the headstones to join her. Side by side they went through the lychgate and down the street towards the stream.

There are now over 500 Puffins to choose from, and some of them are described on the following pages.

Turi's Papa

Elizabeth Borton de Treviño

The future in Hungary seems bleak, but a letter comes offering Turi's papa a position at Cremona in Italy and, penniless though they both are, they decide to set out on foot towards a new life. On the long journey across Hungary, through Yugoslavia and finally into Italy – without identification papers required at the borders – Turi needs to use his gypsy secrets and skills, and at last they reach the University in Cremona where together they find a home and happiness. We share their life and difficulties, and learn a lot about a fascinating race of people.

Based on a true incident, this is a book which will appeal to readers of ten and over who like to discover new places and customs.

The White Doe

Richard Church

Billy was going away to boarding school, and Tom would be staying at home. The boys were lifelong friends, but now it looked as if they had come to the parting of the ways.

But as it turned out it wasn't boarding school that threatened their friendship, but brash, snobbish newcomer Harold Sims, who despised Tom but claimed Billy for his friend. The only thing that made the year bearable for Tom was the lovely doe and her little white fawn that he had befriended in the winter. No wonder that in the end Harold's decision to hunt the two deer brought the boys' hostility to a life-or-death climax.

This serious character study, told with all Richard Church's familiar skill, is deepened and enriched by the passing of the seasons in the woodland setting.

Also in Puffins by the same author, *The Cave*.

A Handful of Thieves

Nina Bawden

Sid believed that Mr Gribble was sinister the very first time he saw him flapping down Station Road in his big, baggy macintosh. It was something to do with his thin, sad face and his rich, fat voice. But Fred thought his Gran's new lodger was strange because of his extraordinary diet of Hubbel's Fluid, which tasted remarkably like fish glue.

But both Fred and Sid had more important things to think about anyway. First there was the Cemetery Committee. Then there was the Fireworks Fund, which they kept hidden in the wreck of an old Humber saloon. But after the firework party at Gran's, which went suddenly and splendidly right, everything went horribly wrong. All Gran's savings disappeared, together with the mysterious Mr Gribble. In true Committee style, Fred and his friends decided to track down the thief, which entailed taking the law into their own hands and becoming thieves themselves.

For ages nine to twelve, boys and girls.

On the Run

Nina Bawden

It is not very easy to help two entirely different people to run away from home at the same time, but that is what 11-year-old Ben Mallory had to do when, during his stay in London, he went off exploring and made two unexpected friends who couldn't, he realized, be left to fend for themselves. Not content with evading the dangerous political enemies of Thomas's father (who was an exiled East African Prime Minister), Ben found himself saddled with nine-year-old Lil as well, who was on the run from 'The Welfare'.

An adventure that is all the more exciting because it could really have happened. For readers of ten to thirteen.

Let the Balloon Go

Ivan Southall

John Sumner is 12 and lives outside Melbourne. He has the normal healthy wish to play games and climb and swim like any other boy, but he is a spastic, his body won't always do what he wants it to, and an over-anxious mother and well intentioned friends are driving him mad with frustration. Sometimes he thought he would explode – didn't they know that a balloon was not a balloon until someone cut the string?

This story tells how for the first time ever John is left alone at home for the whole day – free to do all those things he wants to do because there is no one to tell him that he can't do them. How many of us would be brave enough to do what John does?

The Runaway Settlers

Elsie Locke

The true story of an Australian family who ran away to New Zealand and became pioneers. They had to go – it was the only thing to do with a father as drunken and brutal as theirs – so Mrs Small and her six children, left their farm in New South Wales, changed their name to Phipps, and sailed away secretly.

The family's adventures with wild pigs and Maoris, the gold rushes which beckoned the eldest son Bill to try his luck, and Mrs Phipps' daring journey through the Southern Alps with a herd of cattle for sale, make this a story that will long be remembered. It also conjures up a vivid picture of New Zealand in the middle of the nineteenth century.

For readers of ten upwards.